Signs of
Life, Love,
and
Other
Miracles

Heartfelt stories of
hope and inspiration

Stephanie Ager Kirz

SIGNS OF LIFE, LOVE, AND OTHER MIRACLES

First Edition Printing December, 2015

Copyright ©2016 by Stephanie Ager Kirz

All rights reserved.

Library of Congress Cataloging-in-Publication Data in progress.

ISBN 978-0-9741027-6-4

Published by White Dog Press, Ltd

321 High School Rd NE #393

Bainbridge Island, Washington 98110

www.WhiteDogPress.com

www.StephanieKirz.com

Designed by Jeanette Alexander Graphic Design

Printed by Lightning Source, USA

TO HOWARD

Dedication

My life is full of miracles. This book is a miracle thanks to all the exceptional people who appeared serendipitously in my life to help me tell this story. Without them and their inspiring experiences, my journey would have been fruitless.

I dedicate this book to my late husband Howard Kirz who always believed in me, even when I didn't.

I also dedicate it to all the blessed souls who came into my life at just the right moment to share this book with you. Thank YOU for joining me on this path and being a miracle, too.

SIGNS OF LIFE, LOVE, AND OTHER MIRACLES

Contents

SIGNS OF LIFE, LOVE, AND OTHER MIRACLES

Signs of
Life, Love,
and
Other
Miracles

SIGNS OF LIFE, LOVE, AND OTHER MIRACLES

Need for Comfort and Inspiration

One August morning, my late husband Howard was about to leave the house at 7 a.m. to go bicycling with friends around Vashon Island, across from Seattle. I had shouted from our bedroom, "Goodbye, honey. See you for happy hour. I love you."

He never came home. While bicycling up a hill, he suddenly dropped dead of a heart attack.

Several days after Howard died, I was standing at the kitchen sink like a mummy entombed in grief, and I heard him say, "Just get back on your bike." I had no doubt Howard said those words to me. That's exactly how he talked. Just then, my neighbors rang the doorbell and walked in. "We're here to take you on a bike ride." If it weren't for them and that voice I heard, I know I would never have ridden again.

The following Valentine's Day, I sobbed in the Safeway store as I passed by the hearts and flowers. I felt a deep hole in my heart and ran out the electric doors to escape. Suddenly, I heard Howard's unmistakable voice loud and clear. "Just go get yourself a little puppy and call her Valentine." I have this adorable 18-pound West Highland white terrier to this day.

I had never experienced that kind of clear connection before, but hearing from Howard made me curious to see if other people received unexplained messages from loved ones or friends who had passed on. Were there people all over the world looking for a way to feel connected with a lost loved one? Since then, I have traveled to five countries in search of a "sign of life" from Howard. On my journey, I found that I, and so many others, share the same intense questions: Are our loved ones all right? Are they still with us every day? Do their spirits return?

A Storybook Marriage

Howard and I had a storybook marriage. People teased us about acting like newlyweds after decades of marriage. We even wrote a little book for couples called *The Yin and Yang of Marriage, Heartfelt and Humorous Survival Lessons from more than 30 Years Together.* "One of the most essential things about our relationship," Howard wrote, "was that we spent a lot of time together. In the early days when we were both working 60-hour weeks, we'd spend the weekend together. It seems to me it's not so much the activities themselves that have worked for us, but the fact that we've explored our world together and hence have learned and grown together. We started out as good friends a long time ago. Thirty years (and a lot of margaritas) later . . . we still are."

A favorite activity of ours was bicycling. We cycled the vineyards of Burgundy, France, with a client of mine who'd purchased a biking and walking tour company. The trip started a whole new string of adventures including pedaling through Tuscany, Sicily, Costa Rica, China, Bali, and Greece. We cycled along the Danube from Prague to Vienna and toured in Scotland, Ireland, Canada, and of course America.

After I retired from a 35-year career in advertising and public relations, I started travel writing. Gratefully, many of my stories were featured in such publications as the LA Times, Dallas Morning News, Boston Globe, and several travel magazines. Howard took the photos to illustrate my stories and, because of his extraordinary color images, our collaborations at times ended up on the front page of the Sunday travel section. What fun.

The day he declared he would bicycle across the U.S. with no support vehicle and no group, I balked. In fact, bicycling 4,000 miles from Virginia to Washington State was the farthest thing from my mind! But I didn't want him to go alone, so he said that if I trained hard (oh lucky me!), I could go with him. It turned into a trip of a lifetime and another book, *The Complete Handlebar Guide to Bicycling the TransAM*, now in its fourth edition.

Because we were so close, the loss of my dear Howard shattered my world. I had never ever lived alone, not even in college. To outrun the grief, I had to keep moving and never stayed in one place for long. I rarely spent time alone. To this day, I still struggle with the empty evenings, darkness flooding into the suffocating quiet. So I started traveling again and, like our travel experiences together, it changed my perspective and led to writing this book.

SIGNS OF LIFE, LOVE, AND OTHER MIRACLES

CHAPTER 1

Searching for a Mexican Connection

My late husband Howard and I were adventurers; in our 36 years together, we explored more than 20 countries. He loved immersing himself in other cultures by getting up early in the morning and walking the streets of wherever we were. He'd chat with the locals and hang out at the corner café. So when we were invited to stay with friends at their restored private hacienda in lovely San Miguel de Allende, Mexico, I thought Howard would jump at the chance. But no; it was one place he refused to visit. No matter how many times our friends asked us, the answer was always the same. Hanging out in an expat community with more than 10,000 foreigners speaking English turned him off.

My friend Dorothy, also a close friend and work colleague of Howard's, had been to San Miguel many times. She planned a trip there for the celebration of Mexico's largest holiday, Day of the Dead or Dia de los Muertos, on November 1st and 2nd. At the time, she was recovering from the loss of her brother who'd died suddenly in an auto accident. Given my recent loss, would I be interested in going, too?

Howard and I often visited Paris in November, but at this time, I felt too sad to go there alone. Mexico sounded like an appealing alternative. Also going were five friends of Dorothy's, all of whom shared losing a loved one. I agreed to join them, not knowing a revelation waited for me.

Welcoming Souls Back to Earth

Dia de los Muertos is a centuries-old tradition of welcoming souls back to earth. Over a two-day period, the living honor and communicate with their deceased loved ones. It's a huge celebration, surpassing Christmas and Easter in its magnitude. As a recent widow struggling to find my footing in an upside-down world, I felt right at home. After all, I never got to say goodbye to my husband who'd dropped dead of an instant heart attack. Maybe this was my chance.

Curious to know why Dia de los Muertos was such a big deal in Mexican culture, I learned this: "Originally the Day of the Dead celebration can be traced to Mesoamerican and Aztec traditions, over 3,500 years ago in Mexico," explained Carlos von Son, a professor at the National Hispanic University in San Jose, California, as published in the *San Jose Mercury* in 2012.

"The tradition of leaving food, drink, and other treats for the dead was blended with the religious Catholic All Saints' Day celebrations after the Spanish arrived and tried to eradicate the festival. Families set up altars or ofrendas in their homes and decorate the graves of their loved ones. While on the surface, it may look like Halloween, it is much more of a celebration of death," von Son stated.

Returning Spirits

According to the holiday, at midnight on October 31, the spirits of deceased children float out of heaven's gates and return to earth to reunite with their next of kin for 24 hours. On November

2nd, the adult spirits come down to enjoy the festivities, too. I wondered somewhat skeptically if my husband's spirit would come to visit. Is this common knowledge in heaven? Do I need to send him an email reminder? He never wanted to go to San Miguel. Maybe he wouldn't notice.

The legend states that if the souls are well treated, they will provide protection and good luck to their families. No wonder relatives spend days and weeks scrubbing the headstones and decorating gravesites and cemeteries for this festival! Folks set up elaborate structures in their homes and adorn them with festive, brightly colored decorations. They add candles, incense, flowers, and photos of their loved ones. Among the offerings made to the deceased are their favorite food and drink, reportedly to lure them back. One of these foods is bread of the dead, pan de muertos, which is a type of sweet bread that's decorated on the top with bonelike shapes or sometimes angels or crosses for use on the graves or altars.

Some even believe the spirits of the dead eat the "spiritual essence" of the offerings of food, so that even though the relatives eat the foodstuff after Dia de los Muertos, they think it lacks caloric value. That's one way to go on a diet.

Around town were intricately decorated sugar skulls—traditional folk art for the festival—made out of white sugar and decorated with colored icing for the eyes, mouth, and teeth. They were displayed on tables or in shop windows and as lifelike skeletons, some handsomely clothed and hanging in the markets.

Dorothy and her friends had rented a three-story hacienda for the trip, but not knowing the other women, I wanted a modicum of privacy, so I stayed alone at a nearby B&B called Casa Posada Corazon.

On my first morning there, I shuffled down the stone hall to find my morning coffee. "Buenos dias," I said to a member of the staff. Then I paused and thought, "Good grief. How do I even say, 'May I have a cup of coffee' in Spanish? This is embarrassing," I mumbled to my lazy self, knowing Spanish-language CDs were still in my car's trunk back in Seattle. "Oh well, I'll learn Spanish on another trip."

Feelings of Uncertainly

It reminded me that when we traveled, Howard would go out and get coffee to bring back to me while I sat in bed waiting for him. That day, a photo of his smiling face sat beside me in a little heart-shaped frame—a poor substitute. "Where is Howard?" I yearned to know.

Since I didn't speak the language apart from conversing in English while buying trinkets, talking to the maids, and with my friends, I never really spoke to anyone. I didn't want to fall into the "English trap" with all the other expats.

Rising early, one morning I offered to help the kitchen staff get ready for breakfast earlier than scheduled. This got me in trouble with our local tour guide, a woman Dorothy hired, who yelled at me by saying, "That's what servants are supposed to do." In my fragile state, this tiny episode triggered an even more insular experience that threw me deeper into my own sense of loss and loneliness. I remember thinking I'd made a terrible mistake by coming on this trip. Maybe Howard had been right about this town!

The town itself, however, was lovely. I walked up and down the tiny, treacherous cobblestone streets several blocks off the main square in the Park Juarez en route to my group's vacation abode. Ancient, painted wooden doors built practically on top of the street belied the fact that anyone might reside behind them. I rang a bell. The doors swung open to reveal a lush hideaway with its pink stucco walls, a private courtyard, and an entryway reflection pool. The Mexican cook there was making margaritas and guacamole in the kitchen. Things were looking up!

The day before November 1st, we set out to tour San Miguel with our guide. The tour group met on the corner of the palm-lined Plaza Major under the towering pink spires of the Gothic landmark church called La Parroquia. At night, its lighted towers reached up to the sky like beacons seeking angels. Our guide was very knowledgeable about the town's history.

A WORLD HERITAGE SITE

Designated a World Heritage Site by UNESCO in 2008, San Miguel de Allende has become a magnet for artists, musicians, writers, and craftsmen. It's also a tourist destination brimming with hip boutique hotels, nightlife, and trendy restaurants serving plenty of cerveza and tequila. The prosperity of the early 17th century residents set the stage for colonial mansions, impressive baroque architecture, and local works of art.

During Spanish colonization, San Miguel de Allende became a fashionable place to live for the wealthy families of Central Mexico, showering it with its endearing charm today. It didn't hurt that one of the richest silver veins in the world was nearby in Guanajuato, which fueled San Miguel's growth. An expat once said, "You go to Florida to die; you come to San Miguel to live." That is, except for on the Day of the Dead.

On a side trip before the Dia de los Muertos Festival began, we ventured 150 miles north of San Miguel to a town called Lake Pátzcauro. Its streets undulated with tourists chomping on churros and buying keepsakes for the holiday. A ghoulish theme prevailed. Little children dressed in costumes carried small plastic pumpkins for pesos and candy. Straw, scarecrow-like bodies and spooky hollow skulls swung in the breeze, twirling in unison on strings. They looked like corpses hanging on a scaffold. At least two-dozen stalls showcased these empty, soulless straw figurines as the sun cast dark shadows through their exposed rib cages. Later, I had a nightmare about my husband dying. Were there skeletons hanging in MY closet?

We saw altars everywhere, constructed for the holiday: in hotel lobbies, in restaurants, on the church steps, and in the stores. Carpets covered with all the trappings of a traditional Day of the Dead altar—in technicolor—spilled out onto the streets. The trappings included framed photos, picture albums, articles of clothing, flowers, candies, and toys. Inspired, we embraced the holiday by building our own altar in the courtyard of the vacation home to pay tribute—expat style—to our loved ones.

Planning commenced as I volunteered to make more margaritas for the group. Someone took charge of selecting the right kind of flowers; another gathered the candles and the sugar skulls and skeletons from the bakery. Each of us collected personal pieces of remembrance.

Chapter 1

In Search of a Cigar Store

When I left our group I walked the streets looking for a cigar store, certain that if Howard came back, he would want to smoke a cigar. Without a map, I wandered as if being guided to find the one and only Havana Cigar Company shop in town. I purchased one Avo Robusto and one Arturo Fuente Hemingway cigar, plus a pack of matches to go with his cigar cutter, which I had packed for the trip. Next, all I needed was a shot of good tequila—one for him and two for me. This altar business was rough going.

Later that evening, under the soft glow of the courtyard lamps, we each placed our treasures on the altar. I laid the cigars, cigar cutter, matches, and libation along with his photo in the heart-shaped frame and went to bed, waiting for "signs of life."

The next day, checking out the town's cemetery, I came across a carpet of a thousand golden marigold petals paving the way there. The distinctive scent formed a spiritual route that the souls of deceased family members are said to follow during the holiday. Also called flor de muerto or flower of death, the marigold represents pain and grief in Mexican culture. Because of that, it's used to decorate graves and altars.

MARIGOLDS: FLOWER OF DEATH

The marigolds grown in Mexico have a pleasant smell. "It was a sacred herb of the Aztecs who used the flowers to decorate their shrines and temples. Upon arrival of the Spanish in the early 16th century, the flower took on a whole new significance. It became a living symbol of the Spanish massacre of the Aztec people. The red blood of the Aztecs splashed over the yellow gold the Spanish stole."

I never did like that flower growing in my garden, and now I knew why.

I tracked the marigolds' orange trail of petals, my eyes wet with tears of loss. It led to a large walled cemetery. After stumbling in, I sat sobbing on a blue cement bench as I pushed my back against the protective whitewashed enclosure. Outside the walls, food stalls and street vendors sold fried pork rind, spicy sausages, corn dogs, churros, and assorted trinkets like those found at a country fair.

After Mass, people crowded into the cemetery bringing tubs of golden chrysanthemums, fragrant tuberose, gladiolus, red cockscomb, and something that resembled white baby's breath. A large pizza box balanced on a young man's head while a boom box under his arm played music as he joined the procession of families who entered to sit in vigil for their loved ones. Mothers and daughters carried picnic baskets filled with bottles of Fresca and Coca-Cola, and an assortment of Mexican beers and tequila. An accordion played a peppy tune as strolling musicians sang along. Folding chairs and blankets surrounded the headstones draped with flowers. Meals were spread out on the gravestones as though they were picnic tables in a park. The once-empty cemetery swarmed with children laughing and running between the tombstones, dancing on the graves.

Death a Celebration

I felt somewhat consoled listening to the cheerful voices in Spanish even though I didn't understand a word. I belonged here with them. Here, death was a celebration, not a sorrow. Stated Nobel Prize winner and Mexico native Octavio Paz: "While death burns the lips of other cultures, the Mexican, in contrast, is familiar with death, jokes about it, caresses it, sleeps with it, celebrates it. It is one of his favorite toys and his most steadfast love."

The morning after I laid out the offerings to Howard on our makeshift home altar, I looked for signs that he might have taken a sip of the tequila or a puff on that expensive Cuban cigar. But the items were left untouched. I knew it was silly, but I desperately wanted to see a sign. By participating in this holiday, had I reunited with my husband's spirit in San Miguel, the place Howard refused to visit when he was alive? Had his spirit come back to earth to say hello and let me know he was okay?

Yes, I felt him there with me in that cemetery, especially when that pizza box went by. He might have gone more for the pizza than the cigar I left on the altar!

Oddly, visiting San Miguel de Allende was a life-changing experience. I never knew that other cultures had these kinds of celebrations of returning spirits. It gave me hope that I wasn't alone in wanting a connection—and a reason to believe he was still there for me.

SIGNS OF LIFE, LOVE, AND OTHER MIRACLES

CHAPTER 2

Going it Alone
in Thailand

One single strand of string bound us together: 17 travelers, 32 guardian spirits, four guides, and a Buddhist monk. We all sat waiting on mats in front of the monk.

Before starting any journey in Thailand, a master ageb, or retired monk, is invited to call the wayward spirits together, reuniting them in a ceremony called Bai Sii for safeguarding the traveler.

"The ageb and his helpers will put jasmine leis around your necks and unwrap a ball of twine to encircle the group like a spirit corral. He will chant his prayers to call in the entities who have strayed," said Piak, one of our soulful Thai tour guides who had been doing this for 20 years.

"After he is satisfied that the spirits are assembled, he will take the string and rewind it to make your bracelets, tied on the left wrist for women, placed on the right for the men in our group. You must wear the bracelet at least three days for protection. Don't ever cut it, or it will bring you bad luck," Piak explained.

Our Bai Sii ceremony aimed to protect us during our bicycle tour through the tropical farmlands and jungle forests of northern Thailand from Chiang Mai to Chiang Rai. It would be seven days and 210 miles of mountain biking over the Golden Triangle, a geographic term that applies to the opium-growing region where the borders of Thailand, Myanmar (Burma), and Laos converge. However, our group would stay safely on the Thai side.

One of my favorite Howard sayings was, "We're too old to drink bad wine." Another was, "You don't know if you're going to get tomorrow." He was certainly right about that one.

Howard had a way of empowering me and others to do things we never thought we could do. For example, I never imagined myself cycling across our vast country. But with my spouse's ebullient outlook to inspire me, I knew I could do it. And so I went to Thailand encouraged by his spirit. On many mornings, I pedaled through the rice fields and thought I heard him laughing with joy at being there with me.

This was my first bicycle trip in 36 years without Howard, only four months after his death. We had planned to take this trip together, and I still wanted to see Thailand, so I mustered up the courage to go in celebration of his life. (Well, the idea looked good on paper.)

Backroads, the cycling tour company, helped me book the trip. "I don't want to go with a bunch of guys or too many couples," I had blubbered over the phone to Jennifer, the touring company rep. She searched the upcoming trips and found me the right combination. Over the years, Howard and I had toured Bali, China, Costa Rica, and many other countries with Backroads, so I knew I'd be in good company even if I wasn't good company myself.

After our time with the ageb, we made it back to our hotel. That night, we assembled around the pool and lit fire balloons to send away bad luck. We watched as rice paper domes heated with beeswax candles silently floated up, disappearing into the moonlight.

"This is done for the king's birthday and for many other celebrations," said Ghing, another Thai guide.

We hadn't yet started cycling, but with these meaningful pre-trip ceremonies, the trip was bound to be blessed in many ways we couldn't imagine.

Bike to Shop or Shop to Bike?

Of the 12 women and five men on this bike adventure, I didn't know a soul. It was as Jennifer had promised, though—the group had more single/solo travelers than couples so it wasn't too testosterone-heavy, thank goodness. These people were friendly and open, but surely they noticed my other half was missing—or did they? Couldn't they see the neon sign around my neck flashing "Widow! Widow!"

Sometimes I wished I were invisible.

Several of the women in the group were hard-charging types who raced the guys up every hill, never missing a chance to extend the maximum mileage for the day. One of the women, a Brazilian beauty, had started cycling only six months before the trip. I was somewhere in the upper middle in terms of strength and experience, meaning I was strong but lazy. We were a varied lot of cyclists. But, besides biking, we had one thing in common: shopping.

At the end of one morning ride, our American guide asked if we'd like to check out a custom silk shop in Chiang Rai. He said, "It's a great shop I found on my last trip that makes by hand the most beautiful clothes. They will deliver them the next day to our hotel. The only problem is that you'll have to skip today's afternoon ride. Who wants to go?"

Hello?

I knew if Howard had been on this trip, shopping would be the last thing he'd want to do. But the 12 of us with two X chromosomes raised our hands along with one gentleman, a professional shopper for a chain of family-owned clothing stores. He'd fit right in! Plus we didn't mind missing the technically challenging second half of the day, which included 20 or so miles in the sweltering afternoon sun.

A driver took us in a van, and when we got there, a sunset of colors greeted us as we entered the tiny shop stuffed with racks of jackets, blouses, and scarves plus shelves bulging with bolts of exotic silk. Who knew we could be such savvy shoppers, aiding one another in selections, fit, and color choices, and even assisting in bargaining the price?

Two and a half hours later, we jumped back in our vehicle and headed for happy hour with our purchases. As I proudly carried my bags filled with custom-fit silk jackets, I pondered how these perfectly lovely strangers in my group could have the talent for helping me happily spend my money.

That night after dressing up for dinner, I sat next to one of the couples. But I felt extremely uncoupled; Howard's absence felt akin to losing an arm or a leg. It left a hole in my heart that nothing—not new clothes or food or drink or even friends—could fill.

Thai Spirit Houses

As we rode through the countryside and small villages on our bicycles, we noticed odd miniature dwellings perched on poles at the corner of many properties. Painted in beautiful colors, some looked like ornate dollhouses or Victorian birdhouses.

"No Thai home would be without a spirit house," said Piak, our guide. "Spirit houses are erected to guard the home and property, and the entities must be given offerings of flowers and food to placate their needs. But if bad luck falls upon a family, the spirit house is removed and placed in a spirit house graveyard."

With so many guardian spirits in Thailand, it seemed only natural Howard's spirit might follow me there as well. He had been so full of life, always packing each day to the brim with adventures and his love of teaching and learning. No matter what country we rode in, Howard had a way of getting the locals to tell us memorable stories. He spoke five languages and could make himself understood in many more. Because he could mimic accents using a few perfectly pronounced words, it gave people the idea he was a native wherever we went.

Before each morning ride, I placed a red heart-shaped "cremulate" (necklace of molten glass with ashes) under my bike shirt. I had never heard the word before, but the funeral home had suggested having one made. There was something comforting about having this sacred piece of glass with my husband's ashes to keep me company on this trip.

I admit, it felt odd not to have Howard riding behind me, which he always did. If he went ahead of me, I'd slow down, which meant getting farther and farther behind. Then he'd stop and insist I ride in front of him. I think it was his way of keeping an eye on me so I wouldn't ever wander out of sight. That was unless I was drafting behind him—one wheel length—so we could go faster.

This time, instead of riding alone, I searched for several like-minded travelers and biked with them each day.

The day after our shopping spree, our group rode through the Mae Suai Valley. Dirt roads led us beside just-planted rice and garlic fields up to the hill tribe community of Lahu Village. Along the way, the farmers worked the muddy ponds dredging up the soil to plant the rice for the next harvest. Thais themselves eat an average of 300 pounds of rice a year, and Thailand is the largest rice exporter in the world.

Children followed us through the small village while we learned and listened.

"His Majesty King Bhumibol of Thailand launched a successful crop substitution program to encourage farmers to stop growing opium like the neighboring countries and begin to grow sustainable produce," Ghing said. "Every farmer keeps his own money for rice, corn, beans, and coffee. A family may only earn 40,000 baht, which is roughly $1,136 U.S. dollars, for the whole year. But that isn't much considering a motorbike here costs 35,000 baht. Farmers might leave and go to the big city, but because their language and lifestyle are aligned to the farm, they always come back."

Meeting the Monk

One of our excursions included a rare audience with a Buddhist monk. Hot and dusty, we leaned our bicycles against several trees in the compound and dismounted. Before going into the monk's temple, Ghing instructed us on the right etiquette. Imagine us clad in sweaty spandex and tank tops. We had to cover our legs and arms with shawls and sarongs so we wouldn't offend the spirits inside.

Ghing told us, "It's disrespectful to point the bottoms of your feet toward the Buddha or monk because the feet are the lowest part of the body and therefore unclean. When you approach the altar, you will light three incense sticks and put them above your heart: one for yourself, one for religion, and one for the earth. Make a wish, bow three times, and then put the incense sticks in the sand in front of the Buddha's statue. We believe the smoke from the incense carries your wish."

We took our seats and sat silently as the monk, dressed in a saffron-orange robe, stroked a rotund stray cat at his feet. He sat cross-legged on the floor and looked down. "You can ask the monk any questions you want," said Ghing, who volunteered to translate into English.

"Why are you a vegetarian?" asked one member of the group.

The monk replied, "Buddhists are vegetarians to have less energy for sex, which is stimulated by eating red meat." I wondered if my vegan friends back home had heard about this.

"Why do the temples face east?"

"Our temples always face east to greet the rising sun so our ceremonies can take place in the morning, thus granting everyone a nice day."

"What is the most important concept in Buddhism?"

He smiled. "Be in the moment. Live in the now. Be happy and do good." That made me think about Howard's saying: "You don't know if you get tomorrow." He always said, "Live for today, but plan for tomorrow." He and the Buddhists were on the same page.

Before we left, the monk said he had this one question for us. "What good thing have you done for the world?" Silence. Even now, I'm still working on an answer.

Land of 35,000 Temples

Three-hundred-sixty-five steps, one for each day of the year, led to the top of a temple where a contented-looking Buddha statue sat. Our route took us to a famous wat, which is an enclosure that encompasses a temple, a Buddhist monastery, and a community center. In a land of 35,000 Buddhist temples, we quickly learned that if we steered our bikes under a temple entry gate and rode out under the opposite one, it brings good luck. I made a habit of doing this often.

While trudging down the temple stairs in my slippery cycling shoes, I looked down and saw a silver shimmer of something in the sand. It was directly in my path, but many others had walked right over it. As I reached down to pick it up, I discovered a little heart the size of a quarter with the word "Love" inscribed on the back.

"It's got to be a lucky sign meant for you," said one of the women cyclists who witnessed this.

It wasn't until I got home from the trip that I found a pair of heart-shaped earrings in the back of my jewelry drawer. They were an exact match to the little heart I'd found in Thailand.

In my own heart, I knew Howard had put it in my path. He wanted to let me know he was protecting and loving me on my first solo journey.

CHAPTER 3

In Egypt Does Life Ever End?

Between my incessant wanderings, I hid out in Tucson, Arizona. The dry desert gave me a tonic for grief.

One of my Tucson friends, Lynn, put together a 25th anniversary trip to Egypt for a couple wanting to renew their vows in the King's Chamber, which had a spiritual significance for them. I was, of course, without Howard, but I signed up for the trip hoping the "couple thing" wouldn't undo me. Although hanging out with couples as a single was always stressful, enough singles had signed on to this trip that I took a big chance.

Our leader Lynn, who raised camels in her desert backyard on the Catalina highway, had visited Egypt 18 times. I trusted that if anyone could lead a fabulous tour to Egypt, it was Lynn.

EGYPT: Mummies, Tombs, Scents, and Sand

Like San Miguel de Allende, Mexico, Egypt was a place Howard would never be caught in—dead or alive. I never understood this. I know he didn't believe in reincarnation; perhaps that's why Egypt didn't appeal. I, on the other hand, recalled drawing a mural of elaborate hieroglyphics and a scene of an Egyptian temple from a book as a child. An odd but familiar feeling about deeply connecting with those images came to me. Had I been an Egyptian scribe in a past life (if there was such a thing)?

I was still looking for that answer and many more when I got off the plane in Cairo. We shuttled to Giza and the Le Meridian Pyramids Hotel, aptly named for its spectacular view of two majestic pyramids in the distance. Built some 4,500 years ago, these pyramids served as tombs for the dead kings Khufu and his son Khafre.

That evening I sat poolside with a cool drink and gazed out over these ancient monuments wondering, "Have I been here before?"

Most of my trips with Howard had been active—biking, hiking, and focused on moving. Here, for the first time in my life, I found myself spending hours on an air-conditioned bus driving from temple to temple, tomb to tomb, as though I were encased in a steal casket myself!

Although I never confessed this to my travel companions for fear of putting a damper on the trip, I nearly died from the monotony of the bus rides. So to survive, I started a passionate email exchange with my first true love, my boyfriend from our college days.

"Maybe he was my soul mate and I was having a kind of soul reunion with a lost love," I wondered. I visually remembered the feel of his arms, his mouth, and his kisses. Because I had known him when we were young and innocent, the memory seemed like a safe, wonderful diversion. I wasn't afraid to be loved again.

While stuffed on this Egyptian bus, I fantasied about living with him in Hawaii where he had a winter home. And I dreamed we'd be a couple again as we were in college, feeling so much in love. I imagined my days of living alone and being heartbroken were over, thanks to this perfect (imaginary) fix.

But that was strictly wishful thinking. Poor guy. I had fallen in love with a memory. While on that trip, I even sent him poems, which made me feel even more stupid when he dumped me after I got home. Here's one of the poems:

It's been so long
My tears are frozen in time
I need some way
To unlock this heart of mine.
I need a fix
From your sugar lips
On mine
It's been a long time.
I want those hummingbird sips
Of wine
On mine
It's been a long time.
I need a fix
From your sugar lips
On mine
It's been a long time.

Yes, he must have sensed somewhere deep down I was needy and begging for a solution, any solution, to fill my empty heart. I know; it was way too soon after Howard died to be hooking up with anyone, let alone him.

When we did finally have a reunion face-to-face in Seattle, he proclaimed he was saving himself for a younger woman who could have his babies. He had never married nor had children. I felt a stab in my heart—so vulnerable, so stupid. I had spent a ton of money on Victoria Secret dainties thinking I was going to get laid. (I know that's not stated in a ladylike way, but it's true.)

Oddly, we are still friends, and to this day I'm thankful that he didn't want me in that way. (I admit, a few of my guy friends thought he was crazy not to take me up on my offer.) I will be forever grateful to him for that rejection, which set me free to find me. It was the first of several karmic coincidences that I began to honor in my journey. But, of course, he's still looking for that sweet young thing—and I'm still looking for true love.

The City of the Dead

My obsession with communicating with this past lover left no room for messages, if there were to be any, from my late husband Howard. I was left to wallow in my grief alone and wonder why they called a certain part of Cairo "The City of the Dead." Did the spirits return there as they did in Mexico?

City of the Dead (Cairo Necropolis) is the largest cemetery and necropolis in the world. More than a million inhabitants actually live in tomb houses, working and breathing among these structures built for the dead. Signs of death followed me throughout Egypt, fertilizing my understanding of how other cultures live with concepts foreign to my western world. This necropolis was one example.

But overall, love trumped death on this trip. To celebrate the honored couple's 25th wedding anniversary, our group climbed the interior stairs of the Great Pyramid, the oldest, most mysterious, and largest of the pyramids built for King Khufu in Giza. It's the last of the Seven Wonders of the Ancient World still standing. Lynn had secured a private pass for us so we could be on our own that night. Our group was honored to be allowed inside.

Climbing the steep steps up to the King's chamber was daunting. It's a good thing I don't get claustrophobia because there was no headroom in which to stand. Sweating all the way, I crawled up and down the tiny stone steps on my hands and knees.

For the ceremony, we ascended to the King's Chamber where King Khufu was believed to be buried. According to the Egyptians who believe in reincarnation, his soul had escaped to the afterlife, "ascending to the stars." The pharaohs expected to become gods in the afterlife. In the ancient Egyptian culture, maintaining life after death involved a complex funerary cult that meant preserving the body in a mummy form so the honored person's soul would live on. Even animals were mummified. I remembered that Howard once jokingly said he was going to embalm one of our most beloved dogs! Fortunately, that idea never flew.

Once safely outside the pyramid, I heard in the distance the murmur of a thousand male voices chanting the evening prayer at dusk. That eerie sound blanketed the desert sand, enveloping me as I stood under the full moon and wondered what was next. Our group stood in awe at the stunning emptiness of this historic site. There were no ugly tour buses or shoving people or any signs of tourism present—only us and three imposing pyramids standing as they had thousands of years before. We weren't in the 21st century. It felt like some kind of time travel had transported us here.

Just then, we looked up and saw the bright moon in perfect alignment balancing itself on the point of the Great Pyramid as if to say, "Here's your crowning glory. Thank you for coming to Egypt."

Shop of Sacred Scents

"Do you mind if I smoke?" he smiled.

Gamal sat in front of us wearing his traditional embroidered brown caftan. Lynn had scheduled a private visit with this healing holy man in Cairo, a well-known seer and advanced Reiki master. I wasn't sure what that meant, but I knew he puzzled me. He said he was 42 yet he looked 72 to me. Perhaps he was worn out from people needing his healing, which he gave freely. He would say, "I am totally honest always and my heart gives love to all people from my heart to your heart."

Gamal was sitting in his shop of sacred scents, Sheikh Abdull Perfumes Palace in the Pyramids-Giza in Egypt. Surrounding him were a thousand hand-blown perfume bottles of various sizes and shapes on display as if in a museum. This was his Mecca. As he sat behind a large wooden desk, we got comfortable on soft cushions atop inlaid wood benches facing him.

Gamal began, "I will tell you about the seven scents of the Pharaohs and the seven oils of the seven chakras. But first, do you mind if I smoke?" As he lit his cigarette, his brown eyes scanned our group of ten and he asked, "Do you have any questions for me?" Without waiting for a response, he began his story.

"My family owns the land that grows many of these flowers. We distill and extract only the purest oils for sale in our shop." We looked around to see the room lined in beautiful etched-glass apothecary bottles and jars painted with delicate gold-leaf designs. With hundreds of jars backlit on shelves wrapping around the room, it was like being in an aquarium of sacred oils preserved from ancient time and brought forth into the present day.

The ornate bottles were filled with color: dark red amber for the base chakra, rust-colored musk for the second chakra, golden yellow from the double jasmine for the solar plexus, attar of roses for the heart chakra, amber Kashmir for the throat chakra, sandalwood for the third eye chakra, and pale yellow for the white lotus, the seventh and highest chakra. He talked about what each scent meant and how it can help one's body and spirit.

Gamal lit another cigarette and looked deeply into my eyes. I read his heart; he filled mine. Then I asked him this question: "You said twenty-two years ago you took up this calling. How did it happen?"

"When I was young, my mother had a guest, a very high healer who came to our home. He told her then that I had a gift.

It was my mother, my teacher, who taught and encouraged me to use this gift. But it took me many years to come back to it. She is now gone, but I thank her for her wisdom and her love."

He added, "It is the women who bring all the knowledge and the gifts to us. It is the women who are our teachers."

Reading Souls

Then Gamal went around the room and chose a few souls to read from among us. He prefaced his comments by saying, "I will tell you honestly what I see. And sometimes my honesty gets me into trouble. But I must be honest with you because if I don't tell you what I see, then you cannot fix it. If I only give you the energy, you get a hit, and for a few days, it makes you feel better. Then you go back to what you know because that's an old habit, one that's comfortable. But you are not healed. So I must tell you what is wrong so you can heal it."

Then Gamal told me specifically, "You need the musk oil to put your yin and yang in order. You are too much masculine in your energy. You need to balance the feminine, be a woman, and be female now. The musk oil will help you practice your truth. It will help you meet your needs first by listening to your inner voice. You need to listen to your inner voice and don't hurt yourself."

Odd that he picked up on that. Yes, of course, I felt out of balance. Howard had died several years before, and I had taken on roles—mostly the yang, the fire aggressive role—that required pushing through all the decisions and responsibilities I had to bear solo.

"But why do I need the musk oil?" I asked. Of the seven scents, that was the one I liked the least. It smelled funny to me. "The one you don't like is the one you need the most," he explained. "Because you like the others better, that's why you don't need them."

Then he referred to three women in our group, saying, "You three need to forgive the men in your life who have hurt you . . . you need to open your hearts." I didn't know exactly which women he meant. Was he looking at me when he said that? I think so.

The Gift

Hours later—after serving mint tea and black Turkish coffee in delicate glass cups—he presented us all with a gift. "I want you to have something from me. I don't care if you buy anything; this is my gift to you." His sons hastily unwrapped and presented us with glazed pottery incense burners in which to heat the oils. They were little teapots of clay set on a stand. "You put a few drops in the pot with water and your room will smell like a garden of flowers," he said, demonstrating with a small jar in front of him.

Of course, most of us bought the seven sacred oils and spent a small fortune. The next day we stopped at the shop again to purchase even more. I bought the oils he said I didn't need and then the musk oil to balance my energy. I knew he was right about my having too much masculine energy, but I felt at a loss to fix it. "What did he mean exactly?" I wondered.

As we were leaving the shop, Gamal had these parting words for me: "I am responsible for what I say but not for what you hear." Then he lit another cigarette.

The Egyptian Sand Box

As part of our tour, Lynn had arranged for us to travel with a local guide, Ali, whom she knew from past trips. We were supposed to see the Sphinx with a million other tourists, but we immediately changed our plans to take advantage of this guide's wisdom. He led us away from the crowds and over to a secluded sand dune within sight of the pyramids poking out of the desert.

"Take off your shoes and put your toes in the sand between the second and the third pyramids. There, you will feel the most incredible energy," Ali instructed. "It was where the riverbed Nile ran from heaven. The sand from the stones of the pyramids is like gold—a special healing sand. Pour it through your fingers, and you will feel the energy come and go, come and go.

"Take a few plastic bags and fill them with sand so you can have a sand massage later. When you go to the Sand Way, you will feel the energy. But remember, you must be between the two pyramids."

I threw my sweaty socks and filthy tennis shoes in my backpack so I could walk barefoot. Along the way, I had to hop over camel dung, piles of busy little ants, and remnants of the red granite that lined the King's chamber. When I spotted the perfect sand box for me, I found a place to rest.

Just then, I looked up and once again saw the full moon balanced precisely on the point of the Great Pyramid in perfect alignment. I thought, "This must be a sign that gifts of the universe are everywhere, if only we can see and hear them in the second that they present themselves."

Maybe Howard really was here in Egypt sending me this sign of love and infinite possibilities. Hmmm . . .

After I turned away, I busily stuffed sand packets into my pockets and later in my duffle bag to bring home from Egypt. My most prized possession—a suitcase full of sand—would keep reminding me of Howard's love that I felt on the Sand Way.

To see a World in a grain of sand,
and a Heaven in a wild flower,
hold Infinity in the palm of your hand,
and Eternity in an hour.

– William Blake

SIGNS OF LIFE, LOVE, AND OTHER MIRACLES

CHAPTER 4

The Path to Puglia Takes an Unexpected Turn

By the time I decided to bike in Puglia, Italy, I was feeling confident that life without Howard was possible. It wasn't better; it wasn't worse. It was simply different. But thankfully I was making progress on sorting out a new life for myself.

I'm afraid to say it but girlfriends were few when I was married. With Howard as my best friend, I didn't need them, so this "girlfriend thing" became a whole new experience for me. Then I met a woman named Pam on the tennis court in Carmel, California, who also liked to bicycle. I thought, "Maybe she'd like to go on future bike trips with me." In my most recent biking adventure in Thailand, I had gone with a group of friendly strangers, which was fine, but I preferred having a travel buddy.

Then one day after she'd left Carmel and went back east, I picked up the phone and called Pam. "Are you still thinking about that bike trip in Puglia, Italy, that we talked about?" I asked. Amazingly, she had planned to call the company the next day and make a reservation.

What bizarre timing that I would call out of the blue when I did. She'd been planning to go on this trip by herself for three years but didn't know I was interested, too. It turned out Howard and I had had a bad experience with that touring company on a trip down the Danube, so I'd decided never to book with it again. But the price and dates for Italy were right, and Pam's arguments were convincing. Despite feeling skeptical, I agreed to go, giving myself credit for being a good sport. What could go wrong?

Because I didn't know Pam well, we signed up for separate rooms. That meant in a small way I had control of a part of the trip. Besides, I wasn't about to be in a bedroom with anyone, not after 36 years of sharing one with Howard. Maybe she snored or who knows what. She probably felt the same way about me. After all, she was a widow, too. Her husband had died several years before Howard passed on.

Billed as the "undiscovered coast of Italy," Puglia is at the heel of the boot well off the common tourist path. Fortunately, it's relatively flat, so I knew the bicycling would be comparatively easy and we'd only ride 15 to 35 miles a day. That meant I wouldn't have to train hard to get ready—a necessity on hillier trips I've taken in Sicily or Tuscany. I hate training.

From Shame to Fame in Matera, Italy

Before we started on the main bike trip, Pam and I took an excursion to the town of Matera. One of Pam's friends was an Italian count who had relocated from Italy to the States, and when she mentioned we were planning to visit Matera, he was shocked. "Why would you do such a thing?" the count sputtered. "It's the worst town in all of Italy, and you would never catch me there."

Horrified by his comments, Pam had run to the library to investigate his claims, but she could find nothing to support or dispel his disdain. Besides, we'd already booked our tickets to Matera as part of our pre-tour options.

Located in Basilicata, one of the smallest regions of 20 in the country, Matera is about 60 miles from the seaport and capital town of Bari in the area known as Puglia. Once considered the "shame of Italy," Matera became the "darling" in 1993 when UNESCO deemed it a World Heritage Site. We were about to find out why.

"It's not a beautiful city in the traditional sense," said Anna Tamburrino, our local guide. "I've lived here all my life. And it's so architecturally interesting that Mel Gibson chose the location for his movie *The Passion of Christ*."

HISTORY OF MATERA

Matera is one of the oldest inhabited areas in the world, dating back to Paleolithic times when people lived in natural caves on the opposite side of the town's deep gorge. The only comparable city is Petra in Jordan but, unlike Matera, Petra is strictly an architectural site and has no inhabitants.

The entire town of Matera was evacuated from 1953 through 1968 after a government law passed in 1952 ordered the entire population of 15,000 of the Sassi (cave dwellers) be moved into newer housing. It was also called The Phantom City because it was virtually a ghost town after residents were moved. The Sassi lacked sanitation and hygiene, which showed up as a 50 percent infant mortality rate. Imagine living with animals in a cave with no sewer, a family of 11, and the manure from the donkey providing heat for the cave while giving off toxic gasses. This wasn't a century ago; it was happening during the 1950s.

All the dwellings are carved out of the area's soft tufa rock, as it is called. This yummy-looking buttercream material covers the face of every street, hotel, restaurant, and church. After years of erosion, many surfaces are pockmarked, looking like a teenage kid's bad case of acne.

But this ugly duckling of a town has turned into Italy's shining spur in the country's geographical boot. Once it was swept clean and a sophisticated water-sewage system installed, people were allowed to move back into the town. Today, it's regarded as being fashionably chic with its 2,000 residents enjoying an immaculate transformation of the caves into posh hotels, restaurants, and small homes. The town has numerous churches—20 constructed and seven cave churches carved entirely out of the rock. Since inhabitants were living in the caves, they only had one place to bury their dead; in graves on top of their cave churches and homes. As a 16th-century writer said, it was one of the few places where the dead are above and the living are below.

I have always felt a little uneasy about looking at stone coffins set out in the open air above the ground, and I wasn't keen about navigating around them as we treaded in and out the caves. But I was glad we took this side trip, mostly because it gave Pam and me time to get to know one another. She hoped she'd see her Italian count friend back in the States to say that "this little town that could" is in an architecturally rich renaissance. It deserves to be shared. He only knew the old Matera, not the new. After our pre-tour, we met the rest of the cycling group in Bari at the airport. Then we jumped into the van to Savelletri and checked into our first night's accommodation, Masseria Torre Coccaro, out in the countryside. Masserias are large farm complexes, fortified in the 16th century to protect the inhabitants from marauding pirates. Ours was an elegant converted estate with 800-year-old olive trees, ripening vineyards, a cool blue swimming pool, and some of the best breakfasts ever.

After unpacking our clothes, our group set out on a short warm-up ride. Unfortunately, we had to deal with black limos hogging the dirt country roads, leaving little room for our bicycles. It turned out Justin Timberlake was getting married in one of the large protected estates nearby. This created quite a frenzy including stern-looking security guards with guns, media camera crews, and looky-loos everywhere. Excitement buzzed. We later learned through the national news that Timberlake's wedding spot was next door to our Masseria in off-the-beaten-path Puglia. At least my friends who watched ABC and other network news would have an idea about where I was.

The "Monster"

One night I woke up hearing a strange scratching noise as if something was crawling up the walls. I quickly turned on the light to see a large green gecko or lizard hanging from the ceiling. His beady head pointed down toward the floor and his eyes stared straight at me while I lay in bed. This wasn't good. He could fly off the wall, or even worse, run down the wall and up the leg of the bed to visit me face-to-face.

Okay. Enough. I grabbed the room phone and called the front desk. With no Italian words coming out of my mouth, I stammered, "There's a monster in my room." Or at least, that's what they thought I said. Soon, a lovely gentleman named Enzo appeared at the door with a broomstick as thick as a baseball bat to sweep out the intruder. After that, every morning when I saw Enzo at breakfast, we laughed about his valiant attempt at saving me from the "monster."

Signs of Life in Alberobello and the Trulli

The next day we cycled to Alberobello where the streets are lined with cone-shaped, whitewashed houses called trulli—Puglian stone huts—significant since UNESCO also deemed this town a World Heritage Site.

We leaned our bikes against the van and listened to our Italian tour guide explain how the houses are constructed without mortar. That way, the guide said, these limestone dry wall structures could be easily taken apart to avoid paying taxes to the Kingdom of Naples. (Tax evasion started way back.) The oldest trulli, of which more than 1,000 exist, are found in the Itria Valley in Italy dating back to the 14th century. There, mysterious white chalk marks appeared on the rooftops, apparently either to protect the trulli from evil spirits or to bless the house. We saw a bizarre assortment of Christian, pagan, and astrological symbols painted on the rooftops. On one roof, I stood transfixed looking up at a huge six-foot drawing of a heart and arrow. What did it mean?

I hastily handed my iPhone to Pam and said, "Take my picture, please, with the heart behind me for protection," which she did. Could this be a blessing from Howard, a sign of love, like the heart-shaped pendant I'd found in Thailand? After Howard died, I started collecting heart-shaped rocks. Every time I found one on the ground, I thought it was a sign from Howard just checking in on me. When I saw these huge painted symbols on the rooftops at least three to four feet across, I definitely sensed he was there, larger than life.

Our last day of bicycling was billed as one of the best bike rides in Italy. It took us to the edge of the Adriatic Sea and the coastal town of Castro Marina. I have to say, I felt my bike would fly over the cliffs and soar effortlessly above the azure water. What a dream of a day.

And then I met a drink I couldn't refuse.

After stopping in a little village for a seaside picnic our guides prepared, we ventured into a bar and spotted someone with a coffee drink in a glass cup. Love at first sip. Called affogatto (meaning "drowned"), the drink is made by pouring hot espresso over a scoop of vanilla gelato or ice cream. Such a simple treat, yet it was so tasty, I bought an espresso machine so I could make it back home.

Sad Goodbyes

Our Italian guides were smart, fit, funny, and handsome—so handsome that I had Pam snap a photo of me with one of them. I emailed it to several friends back home so they'd wonder, "Wow, is this your new Italian boyfriend?" Hmm . . . boyfriend? Most of the widows I knew were already remarried, but two years after Howard's passing, I hadn't even been kissed. Getting over him was taking its sweet time.

We said "ciao" to our bikes and drove in a van to Lecce, a Baroque city known as the Florence of the South. Well, this might be overstating it because it lacked the over-the-top gilt-edge flourish of arty Florence, but it was a good stopover until the group left to catch a plane to Rome for an after-trip sightseeing adventure.

We checked into the beautiful Patria Palace Hotel in Lecce. While having breakfast together, people in the group urged me to come with them to Rome the next day. "Why stay here alone?" they asked. Now, if it had been Venice, I'd go in a heartbeat, but Rome wasn't my cup of espresso. So I thanked them for their offer and said I'd be perfectly fine all on my own for one more day in Lecce. Boy, was I wrong.

I hugged and kissed everyone goodbye, including my new travel buddy Pam, as they squeezed into the airport shuttle to catch their flight from Bari to Rome.

As the van pulled away, I felt sad as I waved, and then I went back inside to sit alone in the lobby. That's when reality crashed down on me. Why would I turn down their offer to join them just because I wasn't that fond of Rome? I was really fond of all of them and loved spending time with these new friends. Suddenly gone were the happy banter, the group support, and the sense of belonging. I was once again feeling alone in a strange city. So much for making progress on my own without Howard.

In a Panic to Leave

Feeling panicked, I had to figure out how to get out of there, fast. After frantically calling American Express, I followed a suggestion to escape Lecce that afternoon and fly out of Bari as my friends had done that morning. This involved throwing all my clothes into an already jammed suitcase, checking out of the hotel early, hiring an expensive taxi, changing my ticket, and quite frankly wondering why I hadn't taken that earlier shuttle with the group. What was I thinking?

Unfortunately, I got stuck in a terrible thunder and lightning rainstorm in the Rome airport where no British Air flights were leaving that night for London. Three hundred unhappy families with crying babies and grumpy mothers were all trying to decide what to do, with no options. I thought, "Well, if anyone will fly out of Rome during a storm warning, it's the crazy (love them) Italians."

Leaping across luggage and dodging unhappy passengers, I ran across the airport concourse to book the last seat on an Alitalia flight. Once safely buckled in my seat, I thought about this saying: "Denial is not a river in Egypt." Maybe I needed therapy—or at least a couple of dry martinis before my next adventure.

Yes, I still struggled to live without Howard. It wasn't better; it wasn't worse. It was just different.

SIGNS OF LIFE, LOVE, AND OTHER MIRACLES

CHAPTER 5

Seeking Messages in Wales

A conveniently scheduled travel writer's conference lured me to Wales, a region of the United Kingdom I had longed to visit. Perhaps I'd sample the biking or hiking along the newly finished 870-mile Coast Path or trace my ancestral heritage by hunting for family graves and public records. With my green eyes, brown hair, and freckles, I had a bit of Celt in my blood, and who wouldn't want to be related to a Welsh celebrity such as Catherine Zeta-Jones?

But mainly while there, I not so secretly looked for a medium to attempt to connect with my husband. I could use some help hearing what Howard had to say. Maybe there was someone in Wales like the popular TV personality on the Long Island Medium, who connected people with their dearly departed loved ones.

But first, I found Wales has cornered the market on ghosts.

Wales's Spooky Side

After I had I toured a third castle and country estate and heard yet another story about séances, mediums, and people who channeled spirits, I could touch the "woo-woo" essence of Wales. To my delight, I became hooked on finding out Wales's spooky side.

"This is arguably one of the most haunted countries in the world," said Bob Titley, the affable representative for Visit Wales, our host company. "Wherever you find yourself in Wales, north or south, you will never be far away from a stone-age site. In fact, Wales is called 'the castle capital of the world'. It has over six hundred packed into more per square mile than anywhere in the world. There are haunted castles (some with accommodations), ghostly hotels, inns, pubs, and even dungeons that boast chilling ghost stories."

Was it the long, wet winters in Wales that led people to dive into the paranormal? Was it a genetic predisposition?

Titley had sent me a list of places known to have ghosts as well as a week-long itinerary called Haunted Wales, suggesting this route would help me experience maximum scare value. My late husband was always wonderfully tolerant of my fascination with the supernatural he didn't share. When people wanted to know his sun sign, he would smile and say he was a Virgo with asparagus rising.

Creepy Cardiff

Blustering 70-mile-per-hour gusts swept me into Cardiff Castle in the heart of the capital. The wind added an eerie start to our informative tour and impressive catered dinner. Cardiff

Castle dates back to the Romans in 50 A.D. Lavishly decorated and beautifully restored, the Bute family had converted it into a Victorian fantasy.

Our group climbed 'round and 'round the narrow stone spiral staircase to reach the room that Lord Bute created for embracing the supernatural. This was apparent because of the 12 ornate astrological signs painted in gold leaf around the room. Naturally, I searched for my sun sign—Taurus the Bull—lovable but stubborn, as my husband would mutter whenever I refused to budge.

Our guide told our group that for his séances, Lord Bute used a crystal pendulum that hung from the chandelier in the middle of the room. "It was actually the Third Marquis of Bute who lived between 1847 and 1900 and held crystal vision sessions in the Summer Smoking Room at the top of the clock tower," explained the castle's curator, Mathew Williams. Crystal vision sessions? I immediately imagined a group of Victorian aristocrats gazing into a crystal ball. Later, after creeping down the stairs to an elaborate catered dinner and entertainment in the opulent banquet hall, I wondered what they were smoking up there.

Unfortunately, no ghosts appeared at dinner in the castle that evening.

That Old Black Magic

Treated like royalty, our next adventure led us to a fabulous country estate recently placed on the National Trust list. Tredegar House was once owned by the Morgan family who had started the Jamaican Morgan rum empire. One of its members was also a pirate, leading us to believe that's how the Morgans got into the rum business.

A gentle rain greeted us as we walked through the empty stables and onto the lush estate grounds. A distant bagpiper lured us with the bagpipe's whining notes into the servants' quarters. Some of the ladies in our group were dressed in heels, which unfortunately got stuck in the muck. Yet once we were safely indoors, we were handed glasses of sparkling wine before embarking on our tour through the estate's restored rooms. As we passed into the bedroom of one of the heirs, we were told that he converted to Catholicism but still had a Black Magic room hidden somewhere in the house.

To this day, no one knows where it is.

Back at the Park Plaza Hotel in Cardiff, I couldn't sleep at 2 a.m., so for the fun of it, I jumped on the Internet and typed "spiritualism in Wales." Well, I reasoned, with all these ghosts here, I must need a medium to talk to them. And I'd learned Wales has plenty of them. So I googled "mediums in Wales" and a host of names, photos, and contacts popped up—more than 150 people. Maybe I could find one of them to help me talk to my late husband.

The next day, our merry band of tourists was treated to the loveliest Celtic serenade on the courtyard of the Pencoed House Estate, only eight miles from Cardiff. Before dinner, a fellow traveler and I snooped around the grounds and ran into the owner, Judy Williams. She told us that a ghost lived in the house, that the human remains were supposedly buried under a large granite rock outside, but her spirit inhabited their house.

"Yes, we hired a medium to find out what kind of ghost lived here. We were told that, thank goodness, she's a friendly ghost." We all rushed to take photos of the stone where she was buried, but no ghosts appeared on my iPhone. Good grief, I was really getting hooked on the haunted part of Wales.

The Welsh Psychic Hotline

After a large glass of wine at dinner that night, I mustered up the courage to ask some of the locals, "Do you know of a good psychic or medium?" Amazingly, everyone at my table had a friend who knew one, had hired a medium, or had some experience contacting spirits. A friend of a friend recommended Toby from the Psychic Light, who charged only 32 British pounds for 20 minutes. Is this considered a tax-deductible expense? And how much could I really find out in 20 minutes?

That led to discovering the online Welsh Psychic Hotline. There, I found Lynne Caddick—"officially ranked World No. 2 Psychic," at least that's what the website said. She's also a medium whose online message stated: "The following disclaimer is provided for legal purposes only. Each client has his or her own free will. Your destiny is in your own hands. By law I must state: This service is for entertainment purposes and for over 18s only! I would like to say Thank You for putting your faith in me and my guides to bring forth some of your loved ones beyond the veil to speak with you today." Wow, I'd never seen a disclaimer from a psychic before and was encouraged by the professionalism it conveyed.

I was so ready to be entertained that I jumped online and paid for an email reading, wondering if I had foolishly thrown my money away. And then I waited.

My Stairway to Heaven

I spent my last night in Wales at Ynyshir Hall, a country estate and part of the prestigious Relais & Chateaux hotel group. Someone said Led Zeppelin's lyrics to "Stairway to Heaven" were written nearby up the road in Bron-Yr-Aur, which I later verified as true. I imagined myself writing a love poem inspired by the moody, haunting aura of the place. In fact, both Robert Plant and Jimmy Page, who wrote the lyrics of this famous song, have stayed at Ynyshir Hall.

The song's words haunted me the whole time I was there, so I searched for them online to get a sense of what they meant. Today, every time I hear that song, I think of Wales.

Ynyshir Hall, located about 11 miles north of Aberystwyth near Cardigan Bay, is the proud possession of Joan and Rob Reen. The estate once included several thousand acres, but a previous owner sold 1,000 acres to the Royal Society for the Protection of Birds (RSPB), creating one of Britain's finest bird preserves.

This estate was once owned by Queen Victoria who had established opulent gardens in the 1800s. The grounds were manicured carpets of green filled with heather beds, rhododendrons, Japanese azaleas, and numerous species of plants and trees. Being a weekend gardener, I reveled in the creativity of the plantings as I imagined how Queen Victoria had come to love this spot. In fact, I was so thrilled by this place that I fantasized about returning for an old-fashioned Christmas.

On the way into the estate, we had passed the Ynyshir RSPB Osprey Preserve and saw a crowd of preservationists. There, tourists and members of the media were anxiously awaiting the results of "saving" baby ospreys from the nest. This part of Wales had recently suffered from storms and torrential rain that had flooded the babies' nest, nearly drowning them. A team was sent to rescue the chicks.

Perhaps I might find a preservationist society to rescue me? Did I need to be saved by a search and rescue team for heartbroken widows? Was this hunt for signs of life from Howard a ridiculous waste of time and emotion? Was I still drowning in grief? I shook off these thoughts and wondered how long my feelings of emptiness would last. Someone had said it takes two years, but for me, it's taking much longer.

I learned later that one of the two baby birds had drowned in the nest but the other chick was dried off, warmed up, and put back in its newly dried nest to await its mama. That night at dinner, I met Shirley A. Davies who had come back to Ynyshir Hall for the return of the ospreys and the birth of new chicks. As a fundraising project, she had published a book, *The Lady Returns*, chronicling the return of the "Lady" osprey and her "Laird." The year 2015 marked the Lady's 25-year return to the nest at Loch of the Lowes in Scotland. Shirley, also a widow, had dedicated her life to preserving the UK's treasured ospreys—a species first recorded in Wales during medieval times. It's believed ospreys carry a mystical message of the power of nature.

While sipping champagne before dinner, Joan told us a guest had been desperate to book a room over the Christmas holiday one year. "I must see you," she said to Joan on the phone. "I have something I need to tell you."

Joan recounted the event this way: "We sat up till three in the morning and talked about my experiences here. She said she could see a fair-haired, blue-eyed child running around me, a little girl who would become very special to me. At the time I had no grandchildren, but when eventually my daughter got pregnant, I knew my first grandchild would be a fair-haired girl. Now, I have three fair-haired granddaughters."

That evening, I excitedly opened a 13-page email attachment on my computer from the psychic Lynne Caddick. "This is going to be the longest reading I have ever done!" wrote Lynne. I devoured every page.

Yes, my husband is still watching over me, she told me in her writings: "He brings with him much love for you and says you must not hold back within your life, and he is giving you his blessing. He comes with many fond memories."

Whether or not this message was true, it didn't matter to me. The Celtic love of mysticism and the deep connection to the spirits were enough to make a believer out of me.

"Of all ghosts, the ghosts of our old loved ones are the worst."

– Sir Arthur Conan Doyle

CHAPTER 6

Building a New Life in Carmel-By-The-Sea

As a retired emergency room doc, Howard said he never met anyone in the ER who thought he or she would die that day. So we talked a lot about where we'd each live when the other died.

At the time of our talks, we were living on Bainbridge Island, Washington, in a waterfront home we'd designed to look like a Carmel cottage, where we'd both lived at separate times but never together. Howard had lived in Carmel-by-the-Sea when he was stationed in the Army at Fort Ward in Monterey, California.

I firmly stated I'd never sell our Bainbridge Island home. Howard, on the other hand, said he'd sell the house and move into a high-rise condo in Seattle. We both promised not to make any moves for at least two years after the other one died to avoid making a bad decision. Grief has a funny way of distorting reality, we acknowledged.

A Collaboration

For more than three decades, our homes had been a collaboration of us as a couple—joyful creations reflecting our marriage, our partnership, and the wishes of both of us. All decisions about what to buy, where to locate, what style and size of home, had always been made jointly. I'd never ever had a home all my own to decorate, furnish, restore, and make my own mistakes. For me, moving to Carmel represented a chance to create something totally individual and start a new chapter living in a new environment.

Maybe I'd find relocating would be a bad idea. Maybe I'd get depressed. Maybe I'd change my mind. But a series of unusual events occurred that opened doors and proved to be important signs. Without a doubt, Howard was there to help me find my next home, but I didn't know it until too many odd coincidences occurred.

Carmel-by-the-Sea is the city made famous by Clint Eastwood, who was elected mayor and served from 1986 to1988. People always ask me, "Is Clint Eastwood still mayor?" No, unfortunately. But he has made a huge difference there.

I loved that small town from the first moment I walked its streets at age 17. A paradise for creative spirits, the whimsical fairytale cottages and charming kaleidoscope of art galleries, boutiques, cafes, and historic inns continue to attract visitors from around the world.

It was by chance that I found myself in Carmel as a teenager. Following my mother's disastrous and untimely divorce—is there ever a good time?—she attempted suicide. That's when we took a risk and hastily moved from Bainbridge Island to Carmel Valley where I enrolled in Carmel High School for my senior year.

What could have been catastrophic turned into wonderful events that changed my life. A very lucky place for me, I got a fresh start. That's when the high school newspaper, desperate for an editor of the *Padre*, gave me the job. It was as if a red carpet magically appeared to give me access to the school and the town. Jumping at the chance, I pushed past my fears and terrifying timidity of not knowing a single person. I forced myself to sink or swim. By the end of the first school year, I was still fabulously afloat.

After graduating, I left Carmel never to return except for short visits to see my mother and new stepfather. But the sentimental feeling I had for that lucky place has never left my heart.

Return to Paradise

Several years after Howard died, Carmel serendipitously appeared on my radar again when I happened to play tennis with a friend in Tucson. She mentioned she had a family home in Carmel and would I like to go there with her sometime?

Never having ever been on a girls' weekend trip while married, I stalled, feeling unsure of what to do. Finally, after procrastinating, we set a date and arrived just in time for the annual Pebble Beach Concours d'Elegance. The Concours is a delicious buffet of vintage show cars spread out like a feast along the ocean fairway in front of the Lodge at Pebble Beach. I was suddenly back in heaven.

Like an outlaw running from reality, I had been hiding out in Tucson after Howard died. But during the hot summer months in the desert, the lure of Carmel tempted me to relocate, so I started renting cottages. Finding a place that would take two little West Highland white terriers, my constant companions, was a challenge. But once again, the red carpet rolled out and I was given the keys to the city.

Maybe I should buy a little cottage here. As I entertained that thought, a high school chum recommended her friend and realtor to help me start looking. And look I did. I toured more than a hundred homes in two years, visiting some of the most exclusive enclaves on the Monterey peninsula. What a treat to peek into the homes of the rich and famous tucked behind gated communities such as Pebble Beach, The Preserve high up on the hill, and its neighbor Tehama in Carmel Valley. That's where Mr. Eastwood developed property because, rumor had it, he wanted a place with a golf course so he didn't have to wait for tee times at Pebble Beach's famous golf course.

Never Give Up

Finally, after touring endless homes, I gave up searching for the perfect place to buy. Out of frustration, I called Inge, my realtor and the most patient person I'd ever met. Over a martini at Doris Day's Cypress Inn, I explained, "Inge, I'm giving up. I don't want to waste any more of your time. I'm going to continue to rent." With that, we hugged and kissed and said goodbye.

Three days later, I was driving my husband's black Ford 150 down a side street in Carmel and spotted a For Sale sign. The truck seemed to make a U-turn all by itself. I parked, leapt out of the seat, and ran into a huge yard filled with oak trees. There, more than 100 feet from the street tucked way back was the cutest Comstock-built original Carmel cottage I'd ever seen. Spotting someone inside, I dashed back to the truck, grabbed a flyer, and called Inge back into action. The next day, with my dear friend Judy who was visiting from Kansas, we got to see inside the cottage.

It was a nightmare.

Judy and I peered through the cracked and warped windows and doors. Some of the French doors opened out onto thin air. In one place, the doors hung above a huge blackberry bush located eight feet below with no connecting stairs. Nowhere to go except fall and break a leg!

The kitchen floor was covered in linoleum and the ceiling height was set for a midget. The bathroom was black with mold. The cat's pee stains marked the fir floors leaving a disgusting scent. That was just the beginning. I rolled my eyes and sadly declared, "This is too much work for me." I walked out the door.

In the meantime, despite all of its defects, Judy had fallen in love with the cottage. What happened next might be called a cosmic coincidence.

A Cosmic Coincidence?

I wrote a friend this email describing the event:

After we left the house that I walked away from, Judy and I were looking for another house that was listed for sale in Carmel near 6th and Torres, which this great couple told us about the night before while we were watching the Scottish Bagpiper at Spanish Bay. So yesterday we drove to the corner but couldn't find the address. I stopped the truck in the middle of the narrow road, and we looked up and saw this incredible Comstock fairytale home that was being landscaped. It was right out of a movie set. Just then, coming in the other direction, was a woman in her car. She stopped next to us, rolled down her window, and said, "Can I help you?"

We mentioned we were looking for a house for sale near there. We were obviously admiring the house across the street and asked her, "Is this one a Comstock?" She said yes. She then announced she was the contractor hired to redo the house because PBS was coming to film it for a special on Comstock Cottages in Carmel.

"Would you like to see the original home that Hugh Comstock lived in, which was in mint condition? The owners weren't coming in until the following week," she said. We blinked and the next second, we were inside the home running our hands over the soft, smooth banisters that Comstock himself held as he went up and down the stairs. It was a storybook home. This woman named CJ turned out to be one of the local experts on restoring Comstocks. (It also turned out she had many names, but no matter.)

By now, Judy and I had already been in that little dollhouse house that needed so much renovation. I couldn't stop thinking about that place. It had captured my imagination. And the property was fabulous—no view, really, but it sits on such a big piece of land. (Well, big by Carmel standards. Most houses have only a three-foot setback, which is horribly short.)

CJ of course knew about the house. She had been inside and said it wouldn't be that big a deal to get it up to speed. (That's what they all say!) Anyway, with this cosmic coincidence of running into CJ, I called my realtor to go back in to take notes and do a walk-through with the contractor and her partner. I could hardly sleep last night.

Thanks to my friend Judy—always a believer—and the contractor who appeared out of nowhere, I made an offer on the house. I believe my husband found it for me while I was driving his truck—another sign.

This marked a significant time of throwing myself into building a new life and a whole new chapter without him.

Curtain Calls

Another bizarre coincidence (and some say there are no coincidences) was that the local artist Joanne Mathewson had illustrated and published the book *The Comstock Fairy Tale Cottages of Carmel*, but it was out of print when I purchased my home. Amazingly, my cottage called Curtain Calls was one of the 19 Comstocks featured in that book.

My contractor, who wore several hats, had been negotiating

for more than a year for the copyright to Mathewson's book. Joanne Mathewson, in her 70s, didn't have the money or energy to reprint it and was looking for a buyer. Because she didn't need another project, the contractor passed along this opportunity to me via my publishing company. White Dog Press would buy the rights and help facilitate the deal. Sadly, I never had the chance to meet Joanne Mathewson, who passed away only six months after I had acquired the rights to her book.

I have always felt that buying and restoring both the cottage and resurrecting the book were meant for me. It was, indeed, a lucky new beginning—without Howard.

I've included the write-up that appeared in a local newspaper about all of this serendipity.

THE CARMEL PINE CONE JUNE 13 - 19, 2014

Raising The Curtain On A Neglected Comstock
by Lisa Crawford Watson

In one of his most famous cartoons, Bill Bates depicted a mother seagull admonishing her growing chick as it departs the nest:

"And remember; never on a Comstock!"

Locals got the joke immediately. Even Carmel's birds revere the cottages designed by the legendary Hugh W. Comstock, whose work embodies the early architectural style and quaint charm of Carmel.

Although Comstock did not introduce the fairytale-style architecture to the hamlet by the sea—that credit belongs to Edward Kuster, who established the Golden Bough Theatre and designed and built the Court of the Golden

Bough—Comstock, with some 30 cottages to his credit, was certainly the most prolific, effectively establishing the residential character, which continues today.

Comstock's first cottage was a dedicated dollhouse, designed and built for his wife Mayotta Browne Comstock's popular Otsy Totsy dolls.

The elfin architecture caught on, and soon the demand was high for Comstock cottages big enough for people to live in.

"His small, wood-framed storybook cottages are generally finished in 'Comstock stucco,' with its mixture of pine needles to texture the finish, or with vertical board and batts," wrote author and Historic Preservation Consultant Kent Seavey in *The Comstock Fairy Tale Cottages of Carmel* illustrated and originally published by Joanne Mathewson in 2002, and returned to publication by White Dog Press in 2012.

Door and window frames and, in some cases, the applied half timbering are carved along the edges to give the appearance of rusticity and age.

Flared eaves and undulating ridgelines with wood shingles evoking patterns of thatch enhance the effect.

All are set back on their lots from the street, in natural landscape settings on rising ground, or in swales.

Stephanie Ager Kirz, whose principal residence is a "Carmel cottage" on Bainbridge Island, Wash., but who comes to Carmel when it's cold up north, was looking for a place to restore—both the cottage and herself, after the death of her beloved husband Howard Kirz the year before.

What she really wanted was a Comstock.

"We had been coming to Carmel and renting," says Kirz,

"but I really wanted to buy a cottage and make it mine. Exhausted from not finding what I wanted, I'd already told the realtor I didn't want to look any more. Then I saw a 'for sale' sign. Driving my husband's big Ford 150 truck, I made a U-turn, parked, ran onto the property and just gasped.

"I was looking at a two-story Comstock called 'Curtain Calls.'" Built in 1929 for a reported total of $3,000, Curtain Calls belonged to Constance Ferris, a stage and screen star during the 1920s and '30s, who used the property as her refuge, particularly as she became reclusive in her later years.

Over the years, and through several owners, it had fallen into disrepair. When Kirz got the chance to tour the house, she loved what she saw, but realized she was facing a big project.

"I truly believed my late husband had sent me to see this house, but it was a disaster," says Kirz.

"It had been on the market for more than a year, and hundreds of people had passed it up, and I thought I needed to, as well."

Kirz hopped back into her husband's truck and drove away from the cottage.

As she reached the corner of Sixth and Torres, she believed she had come upon another Comstock. She stopped to ask the woman working on it if this was so. Not only was it a Comstock, but it had been Hugh Comstock's original residence.

THE CARMEL PINE CONE JUNE 13 - 19, 2014

The woman working there, who invited Kirz in to take a look, was Abbey Baker of Abbey Baker Design Build in Carmel, renowned for "historic restorations, coastal renovations, new construction, masonry & stone structures and estate gardens."

Kirz hired her on the spot. And then she went back and bought Curtain Calls. "It was the forgotten gem," says Baker.

"It was so dilapidated and deteriorated. But as we went over every square inch of those burlap walls over pine needles and resin, we had a chance to preserve history. This house has been so lovingly restored. Stephanie is the best client; she really understands what a treasure these Comstocks are."

Kirz was riding a camel in Egypt the day escrow closed on her Comstock.

Once she returned to Carmel, the restoration of Curtain Calls took six months from start to finish, including the guest house, which Kirz named "Second Act," and which was rebuilt on the original footprint, with a refreshed board and batten exterior. Inside, a loft space was framed in a little white picket fence with heart-shaped cutouts. All the "Carmel stone" used in the renovation—a term coined by Comstock—was salvaged from the property.

On the main house, plaster walls were restored and repainted in a soft dove gray.

The kitchen was re-imagined to complement the era and the architecture, and yet serve a contemporary cook. Two tiny rooms became one open, airy space. Doorknobs and other fittings and fixtures were replaced with appropriate vintage finds.

THE CARMEL PINE CONE JUNE 13 - 19, 2014

The original Carmel stone fireplace was preserved, and the original roofer was located and coaxed out of retirement to restore the Comstock-style roof, with its wood shingles and wavy ridgelines.

The cottage was designed and built facing west, with the front door opening to Mission Street, just a block east of Hofsas House Hotel which, ironically, was established by Kirz's stepfather, Fred Hofsas, in 1947. Eventually, the orientation was reconsidered, with an eastern facing front toward Junipero Street. During the recent renovation, fill was brought in to elevate by six feet what was once a cavernous front yard, to create a patio outside French doors. Kirz, having admired the hearth at Mission Ranch restaurant, had a similar Carmel stone fireplace built on the new patio.

"I feel that I am the caretaker, the custodian of the Comstock," says Kirz. "It is my responsibility to preserve and restore what Hugh Comstock created, which contributes to the design whimsy and character that is Carmel. It has been lovely to work with the Carmel Historic Preservation Commission—people who also cherish the quirkiness of it all."

Kirz, who is now in the process of restoring the heritage gardens of the property, is pleased with the preservation of her Comstock.

And it is her company, White Dog Press, which re-released Mathewson's book.

"So many people copy the Comstock style, creating real houses with real closets," she says. But this is a true Comstock cottage, restored in his honor."

— **Reprinted with permission from the Carmel Pine Cone.**

THE CARMEL PINE CONE JUNE 13 - 19, 2014

CHAPTER 7

Signs of Life
and More Miracles

"Be open to the signs. Let them know you hear them.

They are always there for you."

– John Holland

In the process of writing this book, I discovered that seeing a "sign of life" from a deceased loved one or friend happens more often than people realize. But feeling concerned that others will think they are nuts, they're afraid to talk about or share their experiences.

When I heard my late husband's voice or saw a "sign of life" from him and also listened and wrote down so many other people's experiences, I felt immediate comfort knowing "we are not alone." In addition, I would casually mention the name of this book— *Signs of Life, Love, and Other Miracles*—and immediately people would say, "I have a story." Many of them—ordinary people who aren't mediums or psychics—felt safe sharing their stories about seeing or hearing their rejuvenating "signs of life" with me. As a result, I feature a collection of heartfelt stories of hope and inspiration with gratitude.

By reading these stories I've recorded here, I hope you will be more open to seeing a "sign of life" and feel the same sense of comfort that I do.

My hairdresser Mel has lots of wonderful stories, and while sitting in that salon chair, I was a captive, appreciative audience. I would rush home and write them down. One day while sitting in Mel's salon with wet, dripping hair, he told me about a dear client who had died—someone who had always smoked cigarettes.

THE SMELL OF SMOKE – MEL

Twice when I came into the shop, there was the smell of cigarette smoke, even the same brand a client of mine, Carol, had smoked. One morning, a friend of Carol's came into the shop for her 8:30 appointment. I asked, "Do you smell smoke?"

"Yes," she said. "Who still smokes in the salon?"

"Nobody," I replied. "But I think that's your friend Carol just saying hi."

"Well," said the friend, "I'm not a bit surprised. Carol always teased that, after she died, she was coming back to haunt you."

ALBERTA – MEL

One of my favorite clients in the salon was Alberta, a stylish woman of great wit and charm. Mel recounted this dream: I thought I saw her earlier that day in the Plaza, but she had died at age 94. I thought, "That couldn't be Alberta. She's dead." I stared at her for the longest time, not believing my eyes. She looked really good with her "designer hair" (as a friend would say), just like I used to do it.

That evening I was at a restaurant for dinner with my wife. There, I saw Alberta across the room with two friends I didn't know. Our eyes met and she gave me the peace sign, which, of course, Alberta never did. We both got up to walk toward each other, and I told her I saw her earlier that day in the Plaza. "I noticed you staring at me," she said. "I'm going to be here for a couple of days so please come by." I truly meant to stop by her house, but then I realized she was just a ghost.

BILLY – MEL

Billy Duncan came in every Tuesday to have her hair done. One week, a good friend of Billy's booked Tuesday at 2:30, Billy's weekly time. When the door suddenly swung open at precisely 2:30, I looked at Billy's friend and said, "Oh, oh, you're in Billy's chair."

Indeed, Billy had died peacefully the previous Friday night, but out of habit, she had still arrived for her Tuesday appointment. Knowing that it was she who opened the door, we both looked over toward it and said, "Hi Billy."

I was helping my wonderful Catholic housekeeper make the upstairs bed when I mentioned my book about signs of life. Immediately, she told me her story, adding that her family never talked about it because people would think them weird.

Baby Makes Three – Krystal

One day, my three-year-old niece Nevaeh (heaven spelled backwards) woke up from a dream very excited and happy (she was usually grumpy when she woke up) and said, "Mommy, Uncle Danny brought me a baby in my dream." She had never met Uncle Danny but had gone to his funeral several months before with her family. His name had only been mentioned once.

She continued, "At first, I was scared of the baby, but then we played together." Her mother, stunned, was sure the baby was her own unborn child who had died prematurely at six months. Nevaeh would have never known she had an older sister.

Another time, the family left the cemetery after paying their respects to a relative who'd died of cancer. As they were driving away, Nevaeh, in the back seat of the car, started laughing. "Uncle Joey is funny," she said. She had never met him, either.

A story from my tennis buddy, Connie...

Angel Wings – Connie

When I was little, I'd hear my mother and sister talk about what color their angel wings would be when they died. My mother said her wings were taupe and peach while my sister's were lavender and pale teal.

One night I woke up and saw a huge moth in the window. The moon lit up its wings in the exact color of Mother's angel wings. Instantly, I knew she was paying me a visit. On another occasion, I looked up into the sky and saw my sister's angel wings of lavender and pale teal in the fluttering clouds.

In this process I called a psychic I had met in Carmel to ask: "Do the spirits ever die?" This is her reply.

My Grandmother – Camille

My grandmother, who died when I was 15 years old, was a little short lady who'd come to me when I needed help. It's been 51 years she's been gone and I can tell you, her spirit never goes away.

I've heard some people say the deceased disappear after seven years—they have other things they need to do. But that's crap. The spirits come to us when we need them. Even today, whenever I need help teaching a class, my grandmother comes to help.

I was lying on the chiropractor's table when I heard this incredible story about a Jewish family.

HEALING MESSAGE FOR HIS DAUGHTER – WILL

When the father of my wife and sister-in-law Jamie died, we flew to Washington, DC, to sit Shiva for a week after he passed. While visiting, my brother-in-law Tim and I had always volunteered to help around the house and Ruth, their mother, appreciated it. This time, she'd had trouble with the garbage disposal not working. We monkeyed around with that garbage disposal for a week but couldn't get it to budge no matter what we did.

On our last day there, we were all sitting around the table noticing that Jamie was having a hard time with her father's passing. Being the oldest, she had borne the brunt of her father's rages throughout her life. My wife said he used to yell at her and verbally abuse her—behavior that was never resolved before he died.

That last day, Tim and I got on the floor and managed to suddenly move the disposal, which had been bolted to the floor. Oddly, the screws had loosened and the whole unit came free. Under the metal plate we found a piece of paper. Tim read it and then handed it to his mother-in-law Ruth, saying, "You need to read this."

It was a page that came from her husband's journal years before—a journal no one knew he wrote. This single piece of paper had been stuck under the disposal for all those years. It said, "I am so sorry that I was so mean to Jamie. I

love her so much and don't mean to be mean. I am so sorry.
I love her dearly."

*I asked my high school friend Christine, who is quite
religious, if she had any contact with loved ones after they
passed. Christine shared this story.*

THE VASE – CHRISTINE

When my mother had her heart attack, I moved into her
house to take care of her. I slept on the living room couch for
almost five years. After she passed, it took several months to
move all the hospital and personal items out of my mother's
bedroom. But finally, I moved into it.

As a gift, a friend sent me a lovely bouquet in a unique
vase that was square and heavy at the bottom. Because of its
uniqueness, I wanted to keep it, so I put it on the top shelf in
the back of mom's closet.

A week later, I was startled by a loud noise. Eventually I got
to the closet and found this special vase on the floor, completely
intact. My sister, who was living with me at the time, also heard
the crash. Always one for a good pun, she said, "Nice of mom
to drop in."

NOTE: When I asked Christine if she had a sense of an afterlife, she
replied, "I do believe there is a spirit world. I have a sense that the
spirit and the energy goes on forever, although my understanding of
it is very primitive. I don't dream about Mom, but there are times I
have a strong sense of her."

My friends who live on Bainbridge Island love their cats and have adopted many over the years. They were driving home one night and saw a grey kitten staggering across the road. Connie leapt out of the car, picked him up, and they took him home. The cat had cobwebs all over his face and was a mess. While visiting the vet to find out if he had an identifying chip, they were told the kitten was a rare breed from Thailand called a Korat. Here's Connie and Tom's story.

A Cat's Tale – Connie and Tom

We never found his owners, so my husband kept him and named him Elliott. Our other cat Charlie took immediately to Elliott. He became a wonderful playmate, and the kitten totally changed Charlie's life. In fact, Elliott totally changed our lives. We only had him for three months.

However, his seizures were getting worse, so eventually we had to put him down. The vet asked, "Connie, do you want to be with him when they put him to sleep?" I was crying so hard, I said no and drove home. I had such remorse for not being there with Elliott in his final moments.

That night, we walked down to the beach to mourn our loss. While sitting on a log, we noticed a little vessel on the bay—like one of those small boats in Asia or India that carry the dead across the river to be buried. First, we saw one little junket and then a flotilla of beautiful sailboats surrounded by an iridescent light. We both felt the little boat was carrying Elliott's soul to the other side. We just knew his soul was passing by at that moment.

We felt a great sense of relief and gratitude that this cat had brought such love into our lives. Elliott will never be forgotten.

This story came from Jeff, a classmate of mine whom I saw at our 50th high school reunion.

MY DAD'S ADVICE – JEFF

I talk to my father all the time. If I don't have any idea what to do, I ask him, "Dad, what should I do?" The answer always comes from my actions. I don't hear a voice or anything; I just start doing the right thing.

I should have started asking his advice more often. And I really wish that I had taken his advice when he was alive.

My wonderful banker, Ruth told me this heartwarming story over dinner one evening about her nephew, Benjamin, who had died five years before.

FACEBOOK POSTS – RUTH

Benjamin's family keeps up his Facebook page, and every year on his birthday, people still post their messages to him in heaven. A special message came a year after Benjamin's death. His Facebook page received this comment from an old friend: "I didn't know that you were dead until a year later because I was in the military. We still love you and miss you. You'll always be part of my heart."

Linda, who had been married to her husband Dick for 13 years, shared this amazing fish story.

FISHING FOR A SIGN – LINDA

When Dick and I met, we lived on a lake. He had a boat, and we'd go out and sit in the sun, pack a picnic, and fish all day. It was a wonderful way to start a courtship. We both loved to fish. When we found out he had cancer with about five months to live, we talked about some way he could send me a message that he was okay after he died. He passed on June 22nd.

A couple of weeks later, I was driving to work from Lincoln, Nebraska, to Omaha—about 50 miles on Interstate 80 through dry land filled with cornfields. I don't know how it happened but a fifteen-inch fish dropped out of the sky right onto the hood of my car. It was still moving. "Oh my gosh. Dick's talking to me," I thought.

I slowed down but because I was on the interstate, I didn't stop. There was nothing around except cornfields, so I have no idea where that fish came from. But I wasn't alarmed. I thought, "Oh thank you for that. It's exactly what I needed to know you were okay, Dick."

I remember feeling more at peace after that. About six months later, I was at a Catholic retreat and told this story to a priest. I thought he would poo-poo it, but instead he said, "Things like this happen. Don't try to negate it. Don't look for scientific explanations. Accept it as you need to. Accept it as a sign."

I stood in the hallway of my Carmel cottage and asked a
complete stranger if she knew of anyone who might have a
story about a loved one who passed on and then had contacted
him or her through a sign or symbol. She immediately said,
"I do." Here's the story she told me on the spot.

Isaiah – a Caring Neighbor

Five of us had a friend who was dying of cancer. Each day, one of us would sit and comfort her, just be there with her. Toward the last few days of her time on earth, our friend kept saying she saw a man and a small child in the room. Of course, no one saw anyone.

This went on for several more days and finally our friend said, "Isaiah is coming." None of us knew anyone by the name of Isaiah. But for three days right up until her death, she kept saying, "Isaiah is coming."

After the funeral, her closest friend was in a store shopping and saw an adorable baby. She stopped the woman and asked the baby's name. "Isaiah," said the mother. "And he was born on June 9th." The friend stood and stared at the baby, amazed, knowing June 9th was the day her friend had died.

More miracles ...

HOWARD'S ASHES – LOUISE

The day Howard died, I needed to get to Bainbridge Island, Washington from Portland, Oregon (197 some miles) where I live and work, but I wanted to take a shower (I'd worked all night) before I got into my car. I felt him insist I leave immediately, and I remember saying to him, "Back off!" (Yes, I really did yell that at him that day.) He was my big brother and we were very close.

In truth, Howard was concerned about his wife Stephanie being alone and in shock, and I wasn't moving fast enough to suit him. As I was driving to Bainbridge that day, the idea struck me. *That's when I knew he would want his ashes spread in his favorite hiking spot.* As it turned out, he had even specified that in his will, which I had never read.

I definitely got the message that day from Howard and we honored his wishes.

LIGHT WAVES – SANDY

My younger sister died more than 50 years ago when I was only 17 and still in high school. We were very close. She was visiting a family friend when she slid into the pool and touched a metal plate that housed faulty electrical wiring. Instantly, she was electrocuted.

I was in shock. One night, a light in the room awakened me. I would only say it was like an aberration or an aura of my sister. She didn't speak, but I knew she wanted me to know she was okay. That made a huge difference to me to have that contact. Knowing she was all right changed my life.

Love Song – Cindy

Recently, I was in San Francisco with my 12-year-old son Henry to take him to the Sheraton Palace where my husband and I had held our wedding reception 20 years before. I had not been there in at least 15 years.

As I stood in the lobby with Henry, I thought about my father, who had been such an instrumental part of our wedding, and had recently passed away. I looked up to where we had held our wedding party—a room overlooking the grand and historic Garden Court. I was repacking our souvenir bag as we stood at a large table in the lobby that held an enormous vase of red roses.

We had been walking around the first floor for at least an hour and no music had played. But as we prepared to leave, I heard music coming over a sound system—the song Shenandoah. It was the song that, after his passing, I had chosen to accompany the slideshow of photos of my dad's life. It had also played a prominent part in his services.

This is not the type of song that's usually heard at hotels. Mostly they play Sinatra or classical music. And there had been no music playing at all before. Henry looked at me with the same wonder I must have had in my eyes. Rather than being sad thinking of my dad, I could actually smile about it. He was there with me.

Henry and I walked outside a block away to a florist stand and bought flowers for the friend we were staying with. Among the bouquets was a large display with at least 20 single gardenias. I have never seen these at a street vendor's before. Amazingly, a floating gardenia had been our centerpiece on each table at our wedding reception. A cosmic coincidence!

There is a bonding I believe among widows, some kind of secret club that only we share. One of my friends, Pam, lost her husband tragically. She recounted a strange story of his attempts to communicate with her.

MONKEY SHINE – PAM

Because he always called her Monkey, she would draw a little monkey on the napkin that she packed with his lunch. Or she left the little drawing on reminder notes to him if she was gone. Several days after he passed, she turned on her computer and up popped a drawing of a monkey. In fact, every time she turned on the computer, this monkey showed up.

After several months, she tried to get the monkey off her system and even hired a computer expert to figure out why it kept appearing on her screen. With no explanation of where or why it came, they finally were able to remove it. But they never knew how it got there.

Another great tennis buddy of mine, Barbara, said, "My Scottish mother always said she was F-E-Y." I asked her what that meant. "It's the word the Scotts use to describe their E-S-P or intuition about things." Here's her story about intuition.

CALL THE OFFICE – BARBARA

I never thought I had FEY until the day I kept thinking I needed to call my father at his office. The feeling got stronger and stronger and wouldn't go away. It wasn't something I'd normally do, calling him at his office. Instead, I'd phone home and talk to my mother who would then call my father.

But one day, I called Information to get his work number, and then called his office. His secretary answered and said, "Your father is fine. He's in the ambulance headed to the hospital." She assumed I knew. But before I had called, I had no idea he was in trouble.

A story from Amy ...

THE RED CARDINAL – AMY

Years before she died, my mother and I talked about her sending me a sign after she'd passed. I said, "Put a red cardinal on my windowsill, and I'll know it's you. Oddly, several weeks after my mother's sister passed away, a red cardinal appeared on my windowsill. Neither my mother nor I had ever said a word to my aunt about the conversation. But it was like she had heard us and knew exactly what to do.

BEAGLE SIGHTING – CAROL

This book was put to bed, ready to go to the printer's, when I went on a Sunday walk with fellow dog lovers and, once again, just "happened" to hear this wonderful story from a woman named Carol. She had just lost her husband and was in the midst of grief counseling. Stop the presses! There was no doubt in my mind that her tale couldn't wait to be shared. So we redesigned the chapter and added her words below.

At our Westie/Cairn walk today, I related a very odd thing that happened yesterday on Paul's birthday. *(Her late husband's name was Paul Baker.)*

As a friend and I were coming home around Bue Rund Loop, we saw a woman walking a dog down our driveway. We couldn't imagine what she was doing and she walked right into my drive. My friend pulled forward and I got out and asked what she wanted. I thought maybe she was cutting across my lawn to get to Poulsbo Gardens. But she asked if any of us knew the dog she had on a leash. It was a happy, friendly Beagle and she had found it near her home. I leaned over and checked the dog's tags and shockingly, right on its collar was the name PAUL BAKER! I couldn't believe it. There was also a phone number that I didn't recognize and I know his name isn't really uncommon but this was bizarre to happen right on his birthday. I told her I had seen several people walking Beagles over in Poulsbo Gardens so to check there. We laughed about the coincidence and said Good Night.

This morning I was still thinking about that dog and for some reason an old film kept coming to mind. It was about a couple of bachelors who live on the beach. One dies and comes back as a dog. That's when it hit me. Maybe Paul wasn't really coming back as an eagle (as I kept seeing eagles after he died) but rather a beagle! Maybe I just heard something wrong. That dog sure was happy to be in our driveway. I hope that woman finds its owner but I guess I will never know for sure if PAUL BAKER was the owner or the dog's name on that collar. Either way, it was a very odd coincidence to happen on his birthday.

I was at a cocktail party for St. Patrick's Day when one of my tennis partners mentioned her maiden name was Swan. When I said I was researching stories for this book, she told me this wonderful tale.

SWAN SONG – JANET

It was Christmas Day on the Cape, a time of celebration with friends and family with parties and events. But this season, I was sad. Both my parents had passed that year. Then suddenly I saw a pair of beautiful swans out on the lake, and I knew instantly it was Mother and Daddy's way of saying, "Merry Christmas, we are here with you."

Jack, a retired MD, was curious to know what book I was writing
and I mentioned that it was a collection of stories from friends
who had seen or heard a sign of life from a loved one. He patiently
sipped a martini and said, "I think I may have a story for you,"
and the next day, he told me this tale.

WE ARE FAMILY – JACK

My late wife, who was very family oriented, had a favorite song we sang at all family gatherings, picnics, holidays, celebrations: "We are Family." It was only fitting that we all sang her song at her funeral procession.

One day after the funeral, my sister-in-law Madelyn called to say her car was going into the shop for several days. I immediately volunteered my late wife's car—one that she'd loved. It was a 1993 Acura Legend, teal blue green, two-door, sleek vehicle with only 30,000 miles. I had even offered to buy her a new Mercedes, but she wouldn't part with her Acura.

Years before, after their mother's death, my late wife and her sister had become estranged and barely spoke to one another, creating a terrible riff that somehow couldn't be resolved. Just before Madelyn came over to borrow the Acura, I had put out keys and left to run errands. Once she sat down in the car, she started the engine. Immediately the radio came on. It was playing "We Are Family." Madelyn burst into tears.

"It was like my sister was right there with me," she told me.

One of my childhood friends, Marcia, had a brother who was dying, and she told me this story.

Over the Rainbow – Marcia

I had said to my brother, "We all know you're going, so is there anything I can do for you? Call someone? Bring you Oreos?" He replied, "There's nothing because you've already done everything." Then she asked him, "Could you send me a sign that you're okay when you leave? I need to know that you're okay." He asked her, "What exactly?" Without thinking, she said, "Red flowers. Send me red flowers."

After she left the hospice that day, she stopped at a grocery chain to get water. Outside were gigantic red geraniums right out of the greenhouse. As she walked into the store, she heard over the PA system the song "Somewhere Over The Rainbow." She dashed around the store searching for the speakers to hear it closely. Once she heard the lyrics, "Your troubles melt like lemon drops," she knew it was her brother's way of letting her know he'd passed and was fine.

Another story ...

IVORY HEART – MARY

My sister was a nurse who was widowed. A year or so after her husband died, we were doing a big filming job in Hawaii. We asked her to come along to give her a chance to get out of Kansas. She had a good time there, but it was clearly difficult for her.

When she returned home and unpacked her bags, the ivory heart necklace her husband had given her was missing. She tore apart the luggage, called the hotel in Hawaii, interviewed the maids, and talked to everyone she could to find the missing necklace. Weeks went by, and she was still hoping beyond hope it would show up. But nothing happened.

A long time later, she got up one morning and walked toward the dresser where she kept her jewelry. Right in the middle of the floor was her necklace laid out in a nice round circle. It was displayed in such a way that she would have certainly seen it before. She immediately took the sudden appearance of her ivory heart necklace as a sign from her husband.

My sister is a devout Catholic so it's hard for her to go there. But in this case, there was no doubt he had found it for her.

One of my buddies told me this story
after we played tennis one day.

LITTLE BIRD – PATTY

Before my Mother died, she told me that whenever I see a fat little grey bird after she passes, it will remind me of her. She loved birds and had several little bird statues around her house.

One morning after she'd passed, I was sitting on the patio thinking about her, and a fat little grey bird landed right beside me. In fact, seeing the little bird happened more than once. One time I was in Florida on the beach, then in Scottsdale, and also in Tucson. I always knew it was Mother saying hello.

I invited a few friends over one evening and a lovely lady
named Susie whom I'd just met told me this tale.

THE CURTAIN FALLS – SUSIE

The love of my life died five years ago—a wonderful guy. One day, I was standing in the shower and thought, "If you're here, give me a sign." Right away, the whole shower curtain fell down. I thought, "Well, maybe I hadn't secured the rod well enough." So I went out and bought a new rod to hang the curtain on. I jammed it into the wall, tugging on it to make sure it wouldn't fall down this time.

The next day I was back in the shower and said, "If you're here, show yourself." Once again, the shower curtain crashed to the floor. I knew then not to be a doubter. He was clearly reaching out to me.

My artist friend Pablo who lives and paints in Tucson recently purchased a contemporary Southwestern style home that he had admired for over a year. It was owned by a couple who had lived in the house for more than 30 years. Unfortunately, the husband passed away and his wife decided to sell. Pablo told me that something drew him to that house when he walked by every day. So the day the house went up for sale, he called the realtor to see it.

ANNE'S HOUSE – PABLO

It was as if the house were calling me. Even though I had recently bought a place nearby, there was something unexplainable about this house that I loved. I made an offer but several other offers for more money had come in. Yet for some reason, the owner, Anne, wanted me to have her house. I always felt as if I was being chosen by both her and her late husband to be the next owner. Both art collectors, he was also an artist of mobile fish sculptures.

When my sister Carmen came over, we walked around the one-acre property and ended up down by the wash where the river flows after heavy rains. At one point, my intuitive sister stopped in her tracks and started rubbing her arms. She said, "I'm getting goose pimples. There's something here, there's something. You should put a bench here and just sit and meditate. I feel some kind of energy."

As we continued our tour, I didn't think anything about this incident. About two weeks later, I was visiting Anne for coffee.

(The sale of the house hadn't closed yet.) I noticed photos of her and her husband on a desk. Then I asked where her husband was buried. It seemed an odd question, but it just came out of my mouth. She said, "We're not sentimental or religious people so we gathered our family and friends in the neighborhood, walked down to the wash on the property, and sprinkled his ashes there."

Immediately I reacted. "Anne, where? Show me where." We walked over to the bedroom window overlooking the wash, and she pointed to a big white rock lying out there. When I looked down, I realized it was the exact same spot my sister had stood when she had felt the energy.

Without a doubt, I felt that Anne's husband had chosen me to own this house, and that was why I was so drawn to it.

I arrived late and there was only one place out of 21 at the breakfast table. As I squeezed into the tight quarters against the wall and said hello, I casually mentioned the name of my book to Tina, the woman next to me. She said, "I have a story" and without hesitation, she recounted it. After I'd heard this tale, it occurred to me that last seat at the table had been saved so I could meet Tina and write down her account.

High Signs – Tina

I was taking a bath after work one day and suddenly felt my grandfather's presence as he "passed by" on his way to "out of this world." He was flying very quickly on, and I felt no sadness. He simply said to me, "Tell grandma that I love her."

Later that day, my mother called and said, "Your grandfather has died."

I replied, "Yes, I already know."

My mother, astonished, asked, "Who called you?"

"Grandpa," I said. "He came by to say hi."

Thank goodness for Steve! When I'm traveling I have a friend who looks after my Carmel cottage. He shared this story with me over dinner at Il Fiorno and later emailed me the details below.

FRIENDSHIP – STEVE

My friend Rick and I were close school friends from 6th grade on. As we progressed into our thirties, he remained one of my dearest friends. One night in the summer of '93, he sat with my lover and me at our Vermont house overlooking the world on my deck and told us about his terminal illness.

It was a profound year. He died the next summer in July at age 38. I'd spent that whole year with him, but as the time got closer, I bailed. I spent that summer in Italy, which is where I was when I learned he'd died a horrifically painful death.

Even though Rick had passed in July, his memorial was not until the following November. Being of Christian faith, my soul worried for his existence after his departure from this world. I thought of him often; sometimes I worried about him.

The year of '95 was a huge transition year for me, and Rick's memory was far from my mind. But one thing I'm certain about is this: In the middle of the night, I awoke and sat up abruptly and felt this huge presence at the foot of my bed. Unmistakable. It was spiritual and calming. I knew it was Rick; I felt it. I remained sitting up, and the presence conveyed to me, "I'm okay. No need to worry. You may rest now."

At that point I was set free, knowing Rick rested in peace.

I met Marguerite at a Hay House conference in Pasadena where she was promoting her book "Message from Daddy." She said her father sent her a message after his death, which prompted her to write about the many positive aspects of having "signs of life" from a loved one who has passed on. A nurse practitioner and an MDiv in spiritual counseling for more than 40 years, she was kind enough to tell me her story.

A Dream of Red Roses – Marguerite

My father came to me in a dream, almost four months after he died. It was just before Valentine's Day. He handed me a red rose and said, "Make sure your mother knows I still love her." I knew what to do. I went to the florist and ordered a Valentine's Day bouquet for Mother and sent the card from Father. The next day, I called her on the phone and asked her how she was handling Valentine's Day.

"I got flowers from your father yesterday, and I don't know how they got here!" I told her about my dream, and she understood that the flowers were truly from Dad, which made her very happy. I felt blessed to be chosen to give my mother this gift.

Many people shared their wonderful dreams with me.
Here are a few more.

A Dream with Princess Grace – Gayle

My sister passed away in August but her birthday was the 11th of September. I knew Grace Kelly passed away in either August or September. I had this dream or vision: I was asleep in bed and my sister came over and sat on my bed and woke me up. She was with Grace Kelly.

"Leanne… Oh my goodness you're here," I said.

"You can see me?"

"Yes, and I can see that you're with Grace Kelly."

"Yes, and she's taking very good care of me."

Grace Kelly had her hair in braids and wore a white dress. As they went into my closet, my sister said, "We need to borrow some clothes so people won't recognize us." All I remember is one of them took a grey dress while I was standing in the walk-in closet with them. Then they suddenly vanished.

Many years later, I attended an event where I met Albert II, Prince of Monaco. I told him the story about my sister passing and my dream of Leanne being with his mother, Grace Kelly. I asked if he believed in things like that. "Yes, I do," he replied. He didn't think it was strange at all. Maybe he dreams about Princess Grace, too.

Where There's a Will, There's a Way – Gayle

When I was having chemotherapy, I had a dream and went up to heaven where I faced God, right up to God's face. I could feel him. He had beautiful white robes and piercing blue eyes. I was talking into his ear very close to his neck. I could smell him. Beautiful, fresh smell.

I said, "I don't want to be here. I'm not ready." And I willed myself to be back on earth.

A Shopping Cart Dream – Sharon

I had a dream about Bob's mother pushing a shopping cart diagonally across a star-studded sky. Her voice said gently, "I am here for you any time you need me, Sharon. But please take into account it is a long way, and I am very busy." That was all.

Dreamtime Connection – Linda

Eighteen years after his death, my late husband still comes into my dreams a lot. When he appears, I say, "Phil, I'm so glad you're back," and I hug him. Then he says he has to go. He never stays long. But the experience is always homey with feelings of being close. Hugging him makes me feel loved. He was a dear man. We were only married five years, but we still have this comforting connection.

Dreaming and Cruising – Kathy

My aunt came to me in a dream while I was on a cruise in Brazil. She said, "Don't worry about me, I'm here with everyone else." The next morning I received a cable saying she had passed away. Being the last of her family to go, she let me know she was with "everyone else."

Sitting in the dermatologist's chair getting my face zapped
(what we do for vanity), I asked the technician, Brooke, if
she'd ever had a loved one communicate with her after death.
Here's what Brooke said.

Tick Tock – Brooke

The clocks in my house do strange things. Most of the time, they run slow even by a couple of hours. But every time I mention my deceased former business partner's name, something happens with the clocks. We keep changing the batteries and replacing the clocks, but it never fails. If we happen to be talking about her, she seems to mess with my clocks. But there's more to the story.

The first day she came to my office to start working for me, I was nervous and of course running late as usual. She had arrived at five minutes to nine in the morning. When I arrived, she pointed to her wristwatch and said, "You're two minutes late!"

Today, messing with my clocks is her way of staying in touch.

I overheard this story while in a Boston café.

DIMES – COFFEE DRINKER

A brother and sister, who were close, often joked about how they would communicate if either one of them passed away suddenly. "Every time you see a dime, it will be me saying hello," said the brother. After he died, his sister's best friend started seeing dimes popping up in unusual places. The most bizarre one happened when she was running to the bathroom. She pulled down her trousers and—lo and behold—a shiny dime sat in her underwear. Well, that's one way to get into someone's pants!

Chapter 7

The following stories come from my own experience,
which I share here.

Howard's Message – Abbey

As I was restoring the Carmel Cottage (see Chapter Five), I hired a project manager who told me Howard was talking to her! "None of my late husbands ever communicated with me after they passed," she declared, "but Stephanie, yours did! Even though I had never met him, your husband kept me awake for three nights in a row saying, 'If you build that guest house the way it is designed now, she will hate it.' He kept waking me up night after night, very insistent to change the design, which I did. It required eight different permit changes, the most the city of Carmel had ever processed. But we finally made it right, and now it's fabulous. Thank you, Howard."

Alfredo, a colleague and friend of my late husband, wasn't aware that Howard had passed until I called him several months later to invite him to the memorial service. After learning he'd died on August 22, Alfredo recounted a fascinating story about a visit from my husband that day.

Hello Little Brother – Alfredo

I was working in my office that Saturday morning trying to catch up on some projects when I heard a voice coming from the big armchair in the corner of the room. "Hello little brother." I swung my chair around and saw Howard sitting there talking to me. But it was clear that he just wanted to

99

stop by and ask me how I was doing. We talked a bit and then he said he had to go. I really didn't think much about it, but it seems even stranger now, since at the time I didn't have any idea that he was dead.

Especially odd is that my husband had said a year before he died he thought of Alfredo as his little brother, even though they weren't in close contact. Howard felt a strong connection but had never told Alfredo. In this way, he wanted to know if everything was okay.

"JUST CALL MY CELL" – HOWARD

Even after five years since my late husband's death, I was still having the same recurring nightmare about going places with him and then losing him. Unable to find him at the designated meeting place or while out and about, I would get panicky and ask friends if they had Howard's lost cell phone number. They never did. I believed there was no way to reach him without his cell phone number, so I felt helpless and feared I'd never find him.

Of course, in reality he was dead, but in my dreams he was still alive. Then he would just suddenly disappear, much the same way he had died, instantly, of a heart attack. He was simply gone.

After one of these disturbing dreams, the next morning I searched for an unrelated document on my computer and up popped Howard's cell phone number on the screen. It was his way of saying, "I'm here, and you can always call on me. 206-910-1812."

With a huge sense of relief and amazement, I immediately typed his inactive number into my iPhone and knew I could always call on him.

GARDEN PARTY – KARMA

My late husband and I built our retirement home on Bainbridge Island, Washington, where I had grown up. We planted a big natural garden, but in our retirement years we had other things to do than toil the soil, so we hired Karma. Born in Tibet, Karma had walked across the Himalayas and arrived at the border without any documentation. He was a devout Buddhist.

One day after my husband had died, Karma told me he was talking to Howard in the garden. Together, they were watching over the plants. "Really, can you see him?" I asked. "No, but his spirit is there and will be here for seven days, and then it will be time for him to go."

I don't really think he left after seven days. Even after seven years, it still seems like Howard's here for me.

THE BLANKET OF LOVE

I was reading the *New York Times* best seller *Proof of Heaven; a Neurosurgeon's Journey in the Afterlife*. The author wrote that life all boils down to unconditional love and, in fact, just plain love. "Love is without a doubt the basis of everything."

I went to bed that night and woke up remembering my love blanket. What's that? Immediately after my husband died, when I went to bed at night, I'd pull up a blanket of love that would cover me while I slept. People would kindly ask, "Stephanie, how are you sleeping?" thinking I'd be distraught and sleepless. But I knew my husband covered me every night in a most wonderful, protective, cocoon of love. It allowed me to drift off into a peaceful sleep.

At the risk of others thinking I was nuts, I had told a friend who stayed awake all night to "just pull up the love blanket." I haven't used this love blanket in years, but I know if I ever need one, it's always there.

The year Howard died, he wrote this poem for me
on my birthday.

My Diamond

You are the diamond of my life
You are the sparkle in my soul
Your laughter floods my days with light
Your presence warms the nights with gold

I love the radiance in your eyes
The way they shimmer when you smile
And how the glitter in your voice
Makes every precious day worthwhile

Ten thousand dawns I've watched you sleep
Ten thousand dusks of silken hues
Such glorious memories ours to keep
The times flew by before we knew

I love you so my darling wife
You've filled my heart with joys untold
You are the diamond of my life
You are the sparkle in my soul

Always,
Howard

CHAPTER 8

Is This the New Normal?

While writing this book, I heard so many stories from friends and complete strangers about their experiences of having a sign of life, I started to wonder, "Is this the new normal?"

Certainly there are hundreds of books by mediums and psychics who appear to be able to talk to dead people and are featured on television, in movies, and in public presentations. Some of the most famous are James Van Praagh, John Edwards, Sylvia Browne, and the Long Island Medium. But those I talked with were ordinary people. They wouldn't claim to be psychic at all.

Curious to research this subject, I started digging into the Internet past the psychics and made a beeline to the educators and scientists who study what is called ADC—After Death Communication. In this book, I have steered away from this scary-sounding term, and I don't want to perpetuate any frightening aspects of hearing or seeing "signs of life." I share here what I've found to be helpful.

Is Death the End?

First, I found a book called *Love Beyond Life, The Healing Power of After-Death Communications* by Joel Martin and Patricia Romanowski. Originally published in 1998, they were way ahead of the curve on this topic. After hundreds of interviews and years of research, they had compiled a list of how people describe after-death communications. Some of their summaries I found true, while others, based on my own conversations, I saw differently.

They made the following 12 points, with my comments to some in italics.

1. Most people believed that they were the only ones in the world to have had such an experience. (*I found that, with so much publicity in today's media, people commonly know about others who've had these experiences.*)

2. Most people admitted to not believing very strongly in the paranormal, psychic phenomena, or the supernatural. In fact, the vast majority described themselves as initially skeptical or neutral in their opinions of such subjects. Relatively few had expected to have such an experience. Nearly all were surprised when it occurred. (*I found this to be very true.*)

3. Most were reluctant to discuss their direct communication encounters with others, largely due to fear of being misunderstood or ridiculed. Often, one of us was the first—sometimes the only person—in whom the subjects confided. (*In many cases, I was the ONLY person they had ever told their story to!*)

4. Virtually everyone was able immediately to recognize or identify the deceased or loved one coming to them. Some actually saw the deceased, as in an apparition; others smelled a scent or heard a song or sound closely associated with that person. *(It was interesting that many of the people I talked to heard a song that had some connection to the deceased.)*

5. Sometimes the person actually heard the spirit speak, audibly or telepathically. Messages from the dead may also come to us as thought forms, or impressions, that seem to have originated somewhere outside ourselves. Typically, someone will suddenly "just know" or sense that the thought or message came through but not from themselves. Often, a physical sensation accompanies these thought forms: communications like a sudden rush of warmth, the chills, or a surge of energy. *(There was never any doubt from the people I interviewed that the deceased person was immediately recognizable.)*

6. Most communications and visits were from close family members or friends who had died relatively recently, less than two to five years before. Usually the after-death communication occurred within a year of the physical death. However, there are exceptions, as in the cases where a grandparent appears to a grandchild who may not have been born in the grandparent's lifetime. There are also many cases in which a spirit makes repeated contacts over many years.

7. Most often, the contact lasted between several seconds and several minutes, although those that occur in dreams may seem to go on much longer. While many contacts occurred during dreams, the vast majority occurred while the subject was wide awake and fully aware of his or her surroundings.

8. When direct communication contact occurred during sleep, it came as a dream that the subject described as unusually vivid, lifelike, or hyper real. Dream contacts often contain important messages or bring the subject a sense of peace or comfort. Given the content of many of these dream contacts, it seems reasonable to conclude that the spirits choose to communicate at a time when our conscious "guard" is down. History is filled with accounts of such contacts, including several experienced by Carl Jung, who never doubted they were real.

9. In nearly all cases, the deceased loved ones appeared to be in good health, no matter what their physical state at the moment of death.

10. In many cases, the subjects reported their deceased loved ones predicting future events accurately. Sometimes these predictions came as warnings and advice. There is also evidence that those still living but near death can communicate psychically through the same channels as the dead, so that, for example, near the moment of her distant father's death, a woman might feel an otherwise sense of panic, loss, or comfort (crisis alert), actually see her father appear before her (crisis apparition), or hear his voice or telepathically receive a message from him (crisis communication).

11. Religious or spiritual background, or lack of it, seemed to have almost no bearing on predicting who would receive direct after-death messages. Prayer and meditation, however, seemed to facilitate communication, particularly in the first two years after death. Interestingly, such beliefs often

colored the communications' symbolism and language, but not always. *(Some of the more religious people I interviewed were conflicted by what they felt, heard or saw — but it never crossed their minds that the experience wasn't "real.")*

12. Overwhelmingly, those who reported direct after-death communications were grateful for the experience. Nearly all said they were comforted or otherwise helped by it and described it as a positive event. Only a few were frightened or said that they regretted having had the experience. Nearly all said that their direct contact left them feeling "less alone" and that the departed one was "with them." (*In all cases from my interviews, people universally felt a great sense of comfort.*)

I also found *Hello from Heaven: A New Field of Research-After-Death Death Communication Confirms That Life and Love Are Eternal*. Bill Guggenheim and Judy Guggenheim interviewed more than 2,000 people to hear firsthand accounts of spontaneous after-death communication. Their full account of ADC research is available on the website www.after-death.com. (See Recommended Reading for additional books.)

If It's in Mainstream Media, It Must Be True

I started tuning into often miraculous stories featured in the media. Maybe because I was more open to these phenomena, I noticed that mainstream news outlets were carrying unusual stories about communication with the deceased in various forms. Here are a few examples:

KSL-TV—The Voice

I was talking to my friend Terry, a former news director at a radio station where I once worked. He likes to say, "Once a newsman, always a newsman." However, my friends know I rarely listen to the news anymore because there's nothing I can do about all the bad news.

This story became an exception after Terry said, "Stephanie, I forgot to tell you about a story on KSL-TV in Salt Lake City that made the national news. It's about a baby who was saved by Spanish Fork city police officers after they heard a distinctive voice saying, 'Help me.'"

He sent me the links and video, which recounted this heroic episode.

A fisherman, walking the banks of a river, spotted an overturned car out of sight from the road. He immediately called 911. When the police arrived, three of them said they were certain someone was alive in the car because they all heard the words, "Help me."

Rushing into the water, they pushed the car upright and found a baby trapped in the car that had been submerged for 13 hours. For some miraculous reason, the toddler was still alive, although her mother had perished.

The men, shaken by the event and all fathers themselves, said they heard the same female voice repeatedly saying, "Help me, help me." This propelled them to act quickly, and they saved 18-month-old Lily, who has recovered completely.

NATIONAL PUBLIC RADIO—Parallels:
Many Stories, One World

Why I was listening to NPR at that particular moment early in the process of writing the book, I'll never know. But the story's unusual twist caused me to take notes.

According to a story by NPR's Lourdes Garcia-Navarro called "Letter from Beyond the Grave: A Tale of Love, Murder and Brazilian Law," a letter from a murdered victim was channeled from a medium and admitted into court as evidence to exonerate the accused.

The story was so bizarre that the narrator repeated that, "a letter, channeled by a medium, supposedly written by a murdered crime boss to his ex-lover, is admitted in a Brazilian court of law."

According to a Brazilian judge named Padilha De Oliviera, "Ninety percent of the people probably will believe in something; in some kind of spiritual influence. And I think most of the people believe in life after death." He also said, "There are many cases involving spirits in Brazil; you just have to accept it in the process."

The case took place in Uberaba, Brazil, where almost four million mediums practice spiritism. Garcia-Navarro, the NPR reporter, asked the judge, "So if I come with a letter written by a medium from a dead person purporting that this crime wasn't committed or saying that I wasn't the person who did the crime, the judge has to accept it?" Judge Padilha De Oliviera answered, "He has to accept it—the proof—in the process. He can't say, 'Take the letter away from the process' in the process, no, he can't."

COMEDY CENTRAL – THE DAILY SHOW
with Jon Stewart, guest Martin Short

Evenings are hard to navigate for me after my husband's death six years ago. Six years ago? Really, does it ever end? The darkness drops the curtain to daylight, and I'm left all alone. When happy hour comes, I remember getting ready to cook our dinner. Howard would sit in the big wicker chair and read the paper while I fiddled around in the kitchen struggling to do low-calorie cooking. It was a nightly ritual and I miss it.

To keep myself company, I turn on TV. One evening while channel-surfing, I came across Jon Stewart interviewing Martin Short about his new book *I Must Say*. The host was teasing Mr. Short about believing he could still talk to his late wife Nancy, who had died four years before. I immediately ordered Short's book. Clearly, I wasn't the only one who was still talking to someone who had died!

Short had been married to his wife for 36 years. I was with my husband for 36 years, and the time we spent together is so ingrained in me, it's impossible not to still feel his presence. Similarly, in his book, Short wrote about sitting around the lake cabin after his wife passed "waiting for a sign" from her. I thought, "My gosh, he was waiting for a 'sign of life.'" He tells about the wonderful daily conversations he'd had with his deceased wife. Chances are, he is still talking to her.

Why I happened to land on that channel at that particular time while doing research for this book, I will never know. But I believe my husband steered me to that channel. Nice to know he's still around. (Permission pending to use this passage out of the book).

CBS-TV – Sunday Morning

I happened to turn on the TV to one of my favorite shows, CBS Sunday Morning, at the exact moment Stacey Butler was interviewing a young girl who'd sent up a balloon on her late father's birthday every year since he died. She continues to send a letter to her father in a balloon each year so he can read it in heaven. But she'd never had a response.

On this program, she told a heartfelt story about letting go of regret and telling him she loved him. The night before he passed, she saw a call from him on her caller ID but didn't pick it up because she'd been mad at him. She missed the opportunity to tell him she loved him.

But this year was different. The balloon was found 436 miles away by a woman who located the teenager. The young girl said that the woman finding the balloon with her letter was a sign from her father indicating he knew she loved him.

CBS-TV – Sunday Morning

Once again, I was channel-surfing when an interview came on with the publisher of the *Sacramento Bee* whose husband had died. One day, she suddenly saw his handprint on her bathroom mirror. This led to her writing the book *The Hand on the Mirror: A True Story of Life Beyond Death* by Janis Heaphy Durham.

On the first anniversary of his death, a powdery handprint spontaneously appeared on Janis's bathroom mirror. His handprint appeared again on the second and third anniversaries as well. These experiences and many more led her to reexamine the spiritual and pave the way for books such as mine.

Why was I watching at that particular time? Why did this story all of a sudden come into my consciousness? Again, a cosmic coincidence of enormous proportions.

And Then There's Houdini's Promise

However, not everyone is so lucky to hear from the deceased, or maybe they are! This story is widely known and cited among naysayers, but while I was fact-checking, I ran into a different account of how the story ended.

The alleged account of Houdini says that if there was an afterlife, he would send his wife a sign. Thomas Razzeto penned an article called *Houdini's Afterlife Experiment—Did it Work?* in which he documents that Houdini's wife signed a letter stating he'd contacted her in the afterlife with a secret code. However, she later changed her statement so she wouldn't appear crazy.

According to Rozzeto, the story goes....

"Before Houdini died, he and his wife agreed that if Houdini found it possible to communicate after death, he would communicate the message "Rosabelle believe"—a secret code they agreed to use. This was a phrase from a play in which Bess performed, at the time the couple first met. Bess held yearly séances on Halloween for ten years after Houdini's death. She did claim to have contact through Arthur Ford in 1929 when Ford conveyed the secret code, but Bess later said the incident had been faked. The code seems to have been such that it could be broken by Ford or his associates using existing clues. Ford's biographer discovered evidence to this effect after he died in 1971. In 1936, after a last unsuccessful séance on the roof of the Knickerbocker

Hotel, she put out the candle that she had kept burning beside a photograph of Houdini since his death. In 1943, Bess said that, "ten years is long enough to wait for any man."

Rozetto's full account can be found on the internet at www.useyourmagic.com

As you have discovered, my journey started with hearing Howard's voice after he died. Actually I continue to hear him talk to me, or sometimes I get a sense or intuition about some things that I know he wants to tell or show me. This concept was so foreign to me, since it's not readily accepted in our Western culture, that I thought it would be helpful to cite a few anecdotes. I hope that by sharing these excerpts, you too will realize that this experience isn't as weird as I once thought it was. Although I still have some friends who think I'm nuts!

CONCLUSION

What's Next?

Once I started seeing and hearing multiple signs, there was no doubt I had to write this book, but it took me a while to identify the path.

It had started with a few travel stories I wrote that included surprising, unexpected "signs of life" from Howard. But I never knew it would lead me to collect so many inspiring stories from others who had similar experiences to mine.

I didn't have a publisher and I was having a difficult time getting one of the travel stories published. I took it to several travel writing conferences, rewrote the drafts, met with editors, and sent it out again, but no luck. Finally a friend said, "No one is using it because it's being saved for the first chapter of your book!" What book? At the time, I only had a rough idea of what I was doing. Was there enough for the book? Then unexpectedly, all the pieces started falling into place. I told someone it was like I stepped onto a conveyor belt, a moving walkway, like those in airports. And off I went. When I got to the end, I'd walk a little on my own and then step back onto the moving sidewalk, which took me to the next place.

Moving Path of Destiny

When I needed an answer, a resource, a solution to anything, the answer would appear effortlessly. Sometimes I'd hear the first words of a sentence or paragraph, and I'd run for a pen and paper so they wouldn't disappear. The only way I could capture them well was to clear out space in my day—without appointments, interruptions, email, phone calls, texts, whatever might cause me to procrastinate.

This simple, personal process works—except when I stop to wax my desk! What we do to procrastinate! However, when I would turn down offers for happy hour or dinner because I was working, some of my buddies said, "What happened to the fun Stephanie we used to know?"

Toward the end of this process, I hired editor Barbara McNichol, who helped me stitch together the chapters to submit for publication. The publisher was unknown to me at the time, although I dreamed it would be Hay House but in the end, I knew that I needed to take ownership and make it happen myself through my own publishing company White Dog Press, Ltd. With the help of my graphic designer Jeanette Alexander, we captured the chapters which were like floating clouds in the sky, moving here and there, morphing into recognizable shapes out of a few puffs of words into a final, beautiful book. When I finally crafted the ending, I wondered, "Is this just the beginning of a whole new phase of exploration and discovery with more stories and more adventures?" Yes, I will indeed write another book called *Signs of Life, Love, and MORE Miracles*.

There are many more inspiring stories to discover and share.

I'm Just the Messenger

As I described in my Egypt chapter, I feel that I'm the messenger, the scribe, destined to tell the simple story that death is not the end—and that love lasts forever.

Am I still traveling? Yes. I have a long list of places I want to visit, but it's not because I'm restless as I was those first five years after Howard died. Now, I travel out of curiosity and purpose. I want to explore places where cultures such as the Japanese honor the returning spirits of their ancestors in their Bon Odori Festival during the Obon. Pico Iyer, the well-known travel writer, called it the "Festival of Returning Ghosts." That's when floating lanterns are placed in rivers and lakes to guide the spirits home. Much like the Day of the Dead in Mexico, it is a joyful celebration.

Year after year, Howard and I had watched the Kimono and Happi coat-clad participants dance in the streets of Seattle where we lived, but I didn't have a clue about what the dancing meant culturally. I must go to Japan and find out more. How many more cultures around the world celebrate returning sprits? For me, it's like discovering pieces of a treasure map filled with sacred spirits and honored traditions.

When Howard was alive, I'd have a recurring dream that he always got a kick out of. I was riding a pinto pony and served as a scout for the pioneers traveling across the plains. Each morning, I would gallop far into the horizon searching for the best route for the wagon trains and race back to show the pioneers the way.

This sounds a bit goofy, I know. But it's true. Maybe this writing adventure is exactly that. Thank you for coming along on the journey with me. I loved every second sharing this with you.

Please, if you have a story you'd like to share, write me by jumping on my website:

www.StephanieKirz.com

(NOTE: I only use first names, so your privacy is protected.)

Love and Gratitude,

Stephanie Ager Kirz

Acknowledgments

My life is full of miracles. This book is also a miracle, thanks to all the exceptional people who appeared serendipitously in my life to help me tell this tale. Without them and their inspiring stories, my journey would have been fruitless.

Thanks to all the travel writers, editors, travel conferences, and travel partners who kept me engaged:

Maren Rudolph, Travel Classics, for inviting me to join her group of esteemed travel writers and editors in Scottsdale, Arizona, then Quebec and Wales where one of my stories for this book was penned.

Jim Benning who rescued me in an online UCLA travel writer's class and helped me polish my first travel story.

Amanda Castleman who provided structure and constructive editing in her online class.

Barbara Sojourn who helped me understand how to weave paragraphs into a story.

Tim Cahill whose intensive narrative class scribbled an outline on the bulletin board that provided a road map for staying out of the woods.

Thanks to **Book Passage** in Corte Madera, California. If there's one bookstore where you can get the goods on how to travel, write, or photograph, this it. Its gold-plated staff provided me with invaluable weekends full of insights and instruction.

To the book proposal and manuscript editors, thank you. **Anne Cole Norman** who suggested I might have a few more stories in me when I only had three.

Barbara McNichol who wrestled my words into one concise package, which was no small feat.

Mary Liskin, Anthony Valdez, and team from **LMA Film and Video Productions**.

Jon Malecki and **Mike Jones** from **Technivity** for their web development.

Joanna Pyle who graciously agreed to give me a final edit and gave me her seal of approval and lovely endorsement.

Elisa Romeo who generously shared her contacts and experience with me.

Stephanie Ellen St. Claire who is always there for me!

Michael Tucker, Social Mobile Buzz

Jeanette Alexander who has designed several of my books; I will always be grateful for her patience, creativity, and ability to jump on board with an open heart and mind.

To my many friends—you know who you are—and especially to **Jim and Judy Tomlinson**, who patiently watched and waited for the stories to end and this book to be born!

About the Author

Stephanie Ager Kirz enjoyed an award-winning career in advertising and public relations for 35 years. In her retirement, she writes travel articles, which have appeared in the *Los Angeles Times, Dallas Morning News, Boston Globe*, and numerous travel magazines. Her late husband Howard Kirz took all the photos for the stories. Along the way, she created White Dog Press, Ltd., inspired by their two West Highland White Terriers. White Dog Press currently has four books in publication:

- *The Complete Handlebar Guide to Bicycling the TransAM* – Virginia to Oregon/Washington. As avid cyclists, we pedaled 4,000 miles across America and wrote this popular guidebook. Stephanie Kirz, author; photos by Howard Kirz. First published in 2003; now in its fourth edition.

- *The Yin and Yang of Marriage.* Heartfelt and Humorous Survival Lessons from more than 30 years together. Co-authored with Howard L. Kirz. 2011.

- *The Comstock Fairy Tale Cottages of Carmel.* Joanne Mathewson, second edition, 2012. (Copyright acquired and published by White Dog Press, Ltd.)

- *The Lost Book of Fairy Fables.* 2013. A collection of ten original fables as told to a young girl by two ancient fairies concerned with the corrupt and unethical state of the world. Stephanie Kirz, author.

Stephanie continues to write, bicycle, play tennis, and travel in search of "signs of life" from people in cultures worldwide.

Recommended Reading

Alexander, Eden III M.D. *Proof of Heaven: A Neurosurgeon's Journey into the Afterlife.* Simon & Schuster. 2012. Neuroscience meets mystical experiences written by a brain surgeon who risked his professional reputation by writing about his return to life after death. This book opens the door to more widespread understanding of the afterlife.

Dooley, Mike. *The Top Ten Things Dead People Want to Tell You.* Hay House. 2014. Former international tax consultant turned inspirational writer speculates on what the dead are really saying. *Signs of Life, Love, and Other Miracles* goes one step further and documents real people who tell us what the deceased actually have said or indicated.

Durham, Janis Heaphy. *The Hand on the Mirror: A True Story of Life Beyond Death.* Grand Central Publishing. 2015.

Guggenheim, Bill and Judy Guggenheim. *Hello from Heaven: A New Field of Research-After-Death / Death Communication Confirms That Life and Love Are Eternal.* Bantam. 1997.

Martin, Joel and Patricia Romanowski. *Love Beyond Life, The Healing Power of After-Death Communications.* William Morrow Paperbacks. (Reprint) 2008.

Van Praagh, James. *Talking to Heaven: A Medium's Message of Life After Death.* Signet. 1999. I LOVE James Van Praagh and was fortunate enough to see him in action at a Hay House conference in Pasadena, California. While he has written many books, this is one of my favorites. As "an ambassador of the spirit world," he charms his audiences with his wit and insights. He spreads love into the world by sharing his generous gifts from the universe.

Virtue, Doreen and James Van Praagh. *How to Heal a Grieving Heart.* Hay House. 2014. Features practical tips and healing messages with references to "signs of life" from two best-selling authors in a colorful, beautifully illustrated book.

CPSIA information can be obtained
at www.ICGtesting.com
Printed in the USA
FSHW011504100619